Better Homes and Gardens®

CHRISTMAS
FROM THE HEART®

Volume 11

Better Homes and Gardens® Creative Collection™
Des Moines, Iowa

Contents

Sew-up these cozy fleece mittens by the batch for last-minute stocking stuffers and impromptu gift exchanges.

Victorian Splendor

Recollections of Great-grandmother offer the charm of another time to this romantic Victorian-style celebration. With their frills, feathers, and beaded finery, Victorian-era mementos become timeless heirlooms for your family.

An antique cloche, trimmed anew, tops the tree, *above*. Stockings tailored from vintage velvet jackets decorate the mantel, *opposite*. Pretty ornamentals, ranging from a paper village "skirt" to button cards, photo frames, compacts, and purses, accessorize the tree. Instructions begin on *page 14.*

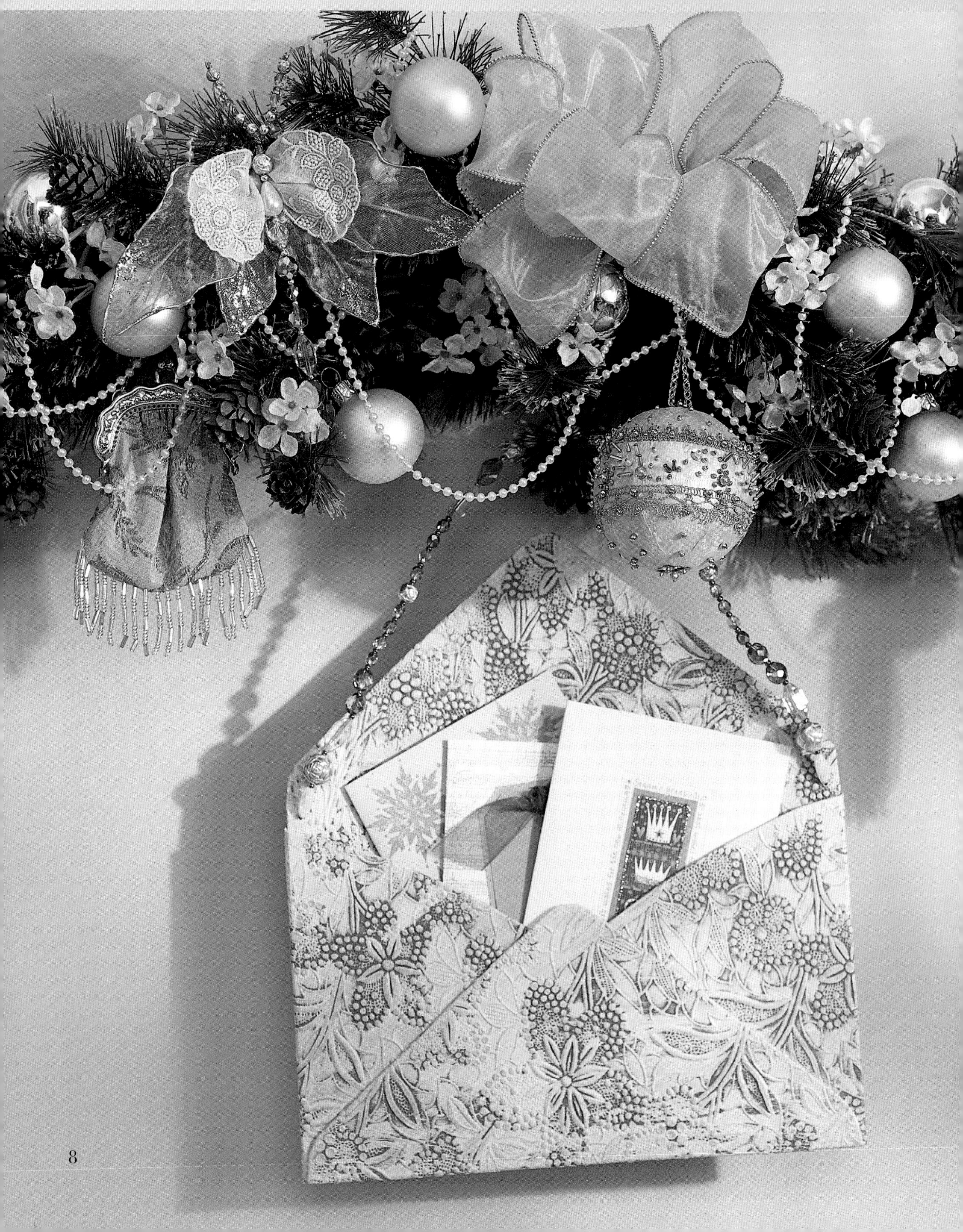

Beaded spirals sparkle like fancy earrings for the tree, *above*. Rummage through jewelry boxes for antique beads first. Then coordinate your precious finds with new ones, if necessary, and thread them onto 18-gauge wire.

A special delivery envelope, *opposite,* is cut from crescent board and covered in embossed paper. Fill it with all your favorite holiday mail, and display it on a doorknob or decorator hook, or drape it from this gloriously ornamented swag. The ornaments (also shown on the tree, *page 7)* are, from *left* to *right:* a metal-clasped purse, crystal-and-lace butterfly, pin-beaded ball, gilded bird, and beaded tassel.

A fantasy butterfly takes flight on wings of silken leaves and crochet, *above*. Start with a doily round from Great-grandma's attic or a piece of new crochet. Add a body made from assorted wired beads. Perch the finished butterfly on the branches of your Christmas tree, atop a package, or in a holiday centerpiece, as shown *above*.

Polish Great-grandma's silver pieces until they're bright and shiny. Then plant the bowls with ruffled topiaries, *opposite*. Shape the topiaries from plastic-foam cones and yards of glittery, wire-edge ribbon.

Like a portrait, this wreath captures the beauty and sentimentality of Victorian times, *opposite*. Adorned in flowers, glittered leaves, berries, and baubles, you'd never know it was newly made. A single glove, bits of jewelry, and a photo tell a story and finish the wreath the way a bow does on a more traditional design.

If you've taken the time to make a themed tree, wrap your gifts to match. This matched pair wears pebbled white paper and vintage corsages, *above*. Decorate another package with the dramatic gold and white tassel, or hang the tassel on the tree.

Victorian Splendor

All projects were designed by Mary Jo Hiney.

Felt Hat Tree Topper
Shown below and on page 6.

YOU WILL NEED
Purchased cream felt hat
Sewing thread and needle
$\frac{1}{2}$ yard of ivory beaded lace trim
3 off-white vintage velvet leaves
$\frac{3}{4}$ yard of 10"-wide off-white hat veiling
Off-white ostrich plume
2—4"–6"-long slender ivory feathers
Transparent tape
2 off-white vintage sequin-beaded leaves
Fancy button or brooch

INSTRUCTIONS
Gather and pleat the hat several times at the center back; sew the pleats in place. Drape the beaded lace trim around the bottom edge on the side of the hat. Sew the trim ends in place. Position one velvet leaf over one end of the trim and two velvet leaves over the opposite end; sew in place.

Beginning and ending at the center back, drape the veiling around the sides of the hat so the veiling hangs slightly off the brim. Gather the veiling ends together at the center back and sew over the pleats. Trim away any excess veiling below the gathers.

Cut the ostrich plume to 6". Arrange the plume with the ivory feathers and tape the ends together. Position the feathers on the left side of the hat's center back; sew in place. Position the sequin-beaded leaves on the right side of the hat's center back; sew in place. Center and sew the fancy button or brooch over the feather and leaf ends.♥

Fur-Trimmed Velvet Stockings
Shown above and on page 7.

YOU WILL NEED
For each stocking:
Graph paper
$\frac{5}{8}$ yard of 44"-wide pale gold burn-out or dusty peach cross-dyed velvet
$\frac{5}{8}$ yard of ivory broadcloth (optional)
$\frac{1}{4}$ yard of ivory imitation fur
$\frac{5}{8}$ yard of pearl trim
6" length of $\frac{1}{4}$"-wide ivory velvet ribbon
Matching sewing thread

INSTRUCTIONS
Enlarge the stocking pattern, *opposite,* onto graph paper. Cut out the pattern piece. *Sew all pieces with right sides together, using $\frac{1}{2}$" seam allowances unless otherwise noted.*

Cut the Fabric
Use the stocking pattern to cut two from the velvet for the stocking front and back. If desired, cut two stockings from the broadcloth for added stability. From the imitation fur, cut a 6×19" strip for the cuff.

Sew the Stocking
Center the velvet stockings over the broadcloth stockings; baste together along all the edges and treat as if one layer. Sew the stocking front to the back, leaving the top edge open. Clip the curves. Press the seam allowances open as much as possible. Press the remaining seam allowances toward the stocking back. Turn the stocking right side out.

For the cuff, sew the short edges together, forming a circle. Finger-press the seam allowances open. Beginning at the seam, pin the tape of the pearl trim to the cuff. Position the outer edge of the tape $\frac{1}{4}$" in from the bottom edge of the cuff. Use a zipper foot to sew the tape to the cuff, stitching as close as possible to the pearls. Fold up the bottom edge along the tape stitching line. Hand-sew the fur edge in place.

For the hanging loop, fold the 6" length of $\frac{1}{4}$"-wide velvet ribbon in half, forming the loop. Baste the ends to the top inside corner on the heel side of the stocking with the loop inside the stocking.

Slip the cuff inside the stocking with the right side of the cuff facing the wrong side of the stocking. Sew the top edges together. Gently pull the cuff away from the stocking; press the seam allowances toward the stocking. Edgestitch around the stocking opening by sewing $\frac{1}{4}$" from the top of the stocking, through the stocking and seam allowance layers. Turn the cuff to the outside.♥

Purse Ornament
Shown on pages 6–8.

YOU WILL NEED
Tracing paper
6×12" rectangle of vintage or fancy fabric
4" length of 1"-wide beaded fringe
Matching sewing thread
2×2½" purse clasp
Sewing needle
6" length of gold chain
2 jump rings
Needle-nose pliers

INSTRUCTIONS

Trace the pattern, *below,* onto tracing paper. Cut out the pattern piece. Use the pattern piece to cut two from the vintage or fancy fabric for the purse front and back. Transfer the marks from the pattern to the fabric pieces. Sew all pieces with right sides together, using ½" seam allowances unless otherwise noted.

Center the 1"-wide fringe along the bottom edge on the right side of the purse front, aligning the tape edge with the fabric edge; pin in place. Hand-baste close to the beads.

Use a zipper foot to sew the purse front to the back, stopping and starting at the dots. Trim the seams. Press the seam allowances open. Turn the purse right side out.

Fold under ½" at the open edges of the purse. Sew as close to the folded edges as possible. Trim the seam allowances. Open the clasp and tuck the purse sides under the clasp hinges.

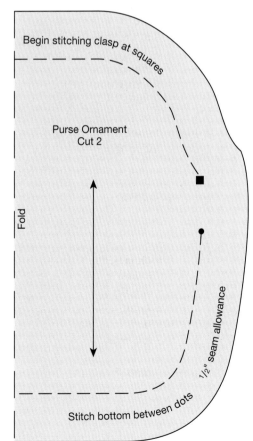

Begin stitching clasp at squares

Purse Ornament
Cut 2

Fold

½" seam allowance

Stitch bottom between dots

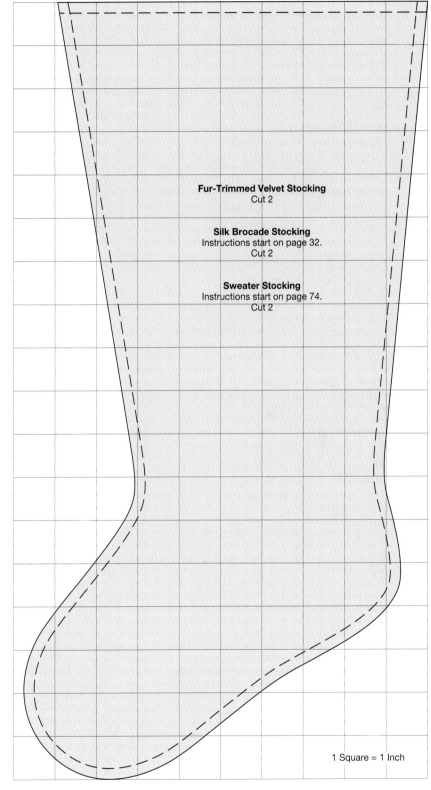

Fur-Trimmed Velvet Stocking
Cut 2

Silk Brocade Stocking
Instructions start on page 32.
Cut 2

Sweater Stocking
Instructions start on page 74.
Cut 2

1 Square = 1 Inch

Thread a needle with four strands of thread; knot one end of all the strands together. Backstitch the clasp to the top edge of the purse front through the clasp holes, beginning at the square marks on the fabric. Backstitch through nine of the holes on the left and right ends of the clasp. Gather the remaining top edge of the purse to fit the clasp and then backstitch the gathered edge to the clasp. Repeat for the purse back. Attach the chain to the clasp with the jump rings, using needle-nose pliers.♥

Envelope Wall Pocket
Shown on page 8.

YOU WILL NEED
20×24" piece of embossed paper
Acrylic paints: ivory and pale metallic gold
2"-wide foam brush
Graph paper
12×30" piece of mat board
3"-wide disposable paint roller
Tacky glue
24" length of 18-gauge copper wire
Assorted colors of round and oval metallic, crystal, and pearl beads: 24 each of 10mm, 8mm, and 6mm, 16 each of 4mm, and size 8/0 seed beads
Wire cutters
Needle-nose pliers

INSTRUCTIONS
Lightly paint the embossed paper with a mixture of ivory and pale metallic gold paint; let dry.

Enlarge the patterns *below* onto graph paper; cut them out. Trace one back, two sides, and one bottom flap onto mat board and one back onto embossed paper; cut the pieces out along the traced lines. Trace one back, two sides (reversing one), and one bottom onto embossed paper; cut out ½" beyond the lines for the flaps.

Use the roller to apply glue to one side of the mat board back. Center the glued side on the paper back with the flaps. Flip the back over and smooth the paper onto the mat board, working from the center out. Wrap the flaps around the mat board. Trim the paper at the corners and clip the curves to the mat board so the flaps lay smooth. Glue the flaps to the mat board. Repeat for the two sides and bottom, but do not wrap the flaps around the mat board at the straight edges.

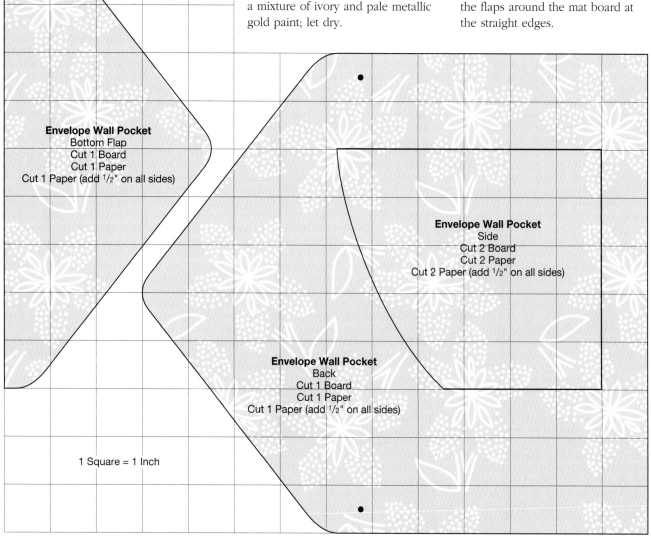

Envelope Wall Pocket
Bottom Flap
Cut 1 Board
Cut 1 Paper
Cut 1 Paper (add ½" on all sides)

Envelope Wall Pocket
Side
Cut 2 Board
Cut 2 Paper
Cut 2 Paper (add ½" on all sides)

Envelope Wall Pocket
Back
Cut 1 Board
Cut 1 Paper
Cut 1 Paper (add ½" on all sides)

1 Square = 1 Inch

Place one side, wrong side down, on the covered side of the back, aligning the straight edges of the mat board. Wrap the paper flaps at the straight edges around the back; glue in place. Repeat with the second side. Attach the bottom in the same manner. To cover the flaps, glue the remaining paper-back piece centered on the back of the envelope.

For the hanger, randomly thread the beads onto the wire, using seed beads to separate the larger beads. Use a wire end or a needle to puncture a hole in the envelope back near each top corner. Insert one wire end through a hole. Wrap the wire end two times around the tip of the needle-nose pliers to secure. Trim the excess wire with the wire cutters. Repeat for the opposite wire end.♥

Pin-Beaded Ball Ornament

Shown above and on page 8.

YOU WILL NEED

3"–3½"-diameter Styrofoam ball
White handmade paper
Mod Podge decoupage medium
1"-wide foam brush
Bright gold metallic paint
Tape measure and pencil
1¹⁄₁₆" straight pins
Gold metallic trims: 12" length each of
  ³⁄₈"-wide and ½"-wide, and 5" length
  of ¹⁄₈"-wide
Beads: approximately 70—3mm gold,
  16—3mm ivory pearls, and 12—3mm
  peach pearls
Seed beads: mauve, platinum, gold,
  and coral
Bugle beads: gold and mauve
Gold sequins
1 large, fancy sequin
Gold metallic small doily or tassel

INSTRUCTIONS

Use Mod Podge to cover the Styrofoam ball with handmade paper. When the paper is dry, lightly paint the ball with gold metallic paint. Let the paint dry.

Designate and mark one end of the ball as the top. For the trim placement, use a pencil to lightly mark around the ball 1⅝" and 2¾" below the top. Use 3mm gold beads and straight pins to pin-bead the ³⁄₈"-wide trim over the top marks and the ½"-wide trim over the bottom marks.

Between the trims, arrange and pin-bead the bugle beads, the gold sequins with pearls, and the seed beads. Angle the pins so that more of the bead shows (and less of the pin heads). Pin-bead the space above and below the trims in vertical lines of gold beads.

For the hanging loop, overlap the ends of the ¹⁄₈"-wide trim at the center top of the ball; pin to secure. Pin-bead a large, fancy sequin over the trim ends. Pin the center of a small doily or a tassel to the center bottom of the ball.♥

Gilded Bird Ornament

Shown at right and on page 8.

YOU WILL NEED

4" white dove
Delicate white feathers
Acrylic paint: pale and bright metallic gold
Paintbrush
1"-wide foam brush
Tacky glue
3 shades of fine glitter
Mod Podge decoupage medium
9" length each of narrow bead trim,
  3mm pearl trim, and strung sequins
Straight pins
2 flat crystal beads

INSTRUCTIONS

Paint the top and underside of the feathers pale metallic gold. Highlight the feathers with bright metallic gold. When the paint is dry, use the foam brush to apply a thin layer of glue to the underside of the dove.

Immediately pour one shade of glitter onto the wet glue; tap off the excess glitter. Let dry. Apply a thin layer of glue to the top of the dove. Immediately pour a second shade of glitter over the wet glue. Tap off the excess glitter; let dry. Apply a coat of Mod Podge to the underside. Pour the first shade of glitter over the wet surface, tap off the excess glitter and let dry. Apply a coat of Mod Podge to the top of the bird. Pour the second shade of glitter over the wet surface. Tap off the excess glitter; let dry. Randomly dab glue on the underside and top of the dove. Immediately pour the third shade of glitter over the wet glue and tap off the excess. When the glue is dry, apply a final layer of Mod Podge. Allow the dove to dry completely.

Glue delicate feathers to the top of the wings and the top and underside of the tail. Glue the narrow bead trim and the sequins around the neck, using the straight pins to anchor the ends. Wrap the pearl trim from the neck front to the back, letting the end of the trim drape off the back; anchor with a straight pin. Pin the crystals to the face for eyes.♥

Gilded Butterfly Ornament
Shown above.

YOU WILL NEED

Gold floral piece with large and small
    fabric leaves
5"-diameter vintage doily
Sewing thread and needle
Tacky glue
Gold glitter
20" length of 18-gauge wire—copper,
    gold, or silver
Wire cutters
Assorted colors of round and oval metallic,
    crystal, and pearl beads: 6 to 8 each of
    8mm, 6mm, and 4mm, and 1—10mm
10—3mm silver or gold beads
Needle-nose pliers

INSTRUCTIONS

Pull apart the floral piece, leaving the
leaves' wires intact. Select two large
leaves for the top wings and two
smaller leaves for the bottom wings.
Twist together the wires of the two
large fabric leaves near the base of
the leaves. Position the smaller leaves
underneath the top wings so the leaves
overlap slightly. Wrap the wires from
the small leaves over the wires from
the large leaves and twist all the wires
together. Separate the wires into two

pairs and twist each pair of
wires together. These will
be used later to attach the
ornament to the tree.

Hand-sew running stitches
down the center of the doily.
Pull the thread ends as tight
as possible to gather the
center of the doily, making a
bow shape; knot the thread
ends together. Glue the center
of the gathered doily to the
center of the wings.

Lightly dab glue onto the
tips of the wings. Immediately
pour glitter over the wet glue,
tap off the excess glitter, and
let it dry.

For the antennae, cut an
8" length of wire with the wire cutters.
Wrap the center of the wire once
around the center of the wings. Twist
the wire halves together as close to
the wings as possible. Randomly
thread eight smaller-sized beads onto
one wire end. Wrap this wire end two
times around the tip of the needle-
nose pliers; cut off the excess wire
with wire cutters. Flatten the cut end
with the pliers. Repeat for the second
antennae. Shape the antennae.

For the beaded body, wrap one end
of the remaining 12" length of wire
two times around the tip of the needle-
nose pliers. Thread an 8mm and a
3mm bead onto the wire and slide
them down to the wraps for the tail
end. Continue to thread beads onto
the wire randomly until the beaded
area measures about 5". Thread on
two 3mm beads and wrap the wire
around the center of the wings from
the front to the back of the ornament.
Slip the wire underneath the center
wrap of the antennae from the back.
Cut off the excess wire and flatten the
cut end.

Hand-sew the beaded body to the
wings between the third and fourth
bead from the top.♥

Spiral Beaded Tree Ornament
Shown on page 9.

YOU WILL NEED

36" length of 18-gauge copper, gold, or
    silver wire
Assorted colors of round and oval metallic,
    crystal, and pearl beads: 20—8mm,
    10—6mm, 50—4mm, and 85—3mm
³/₄" bell-shaped filigree cap
Needle-nose pliers
Paper towel cardboard tube
Wire cutters

INSTRUCTIONS

Wrap one end of the wire two times
around the tip of the needle-nose
pliers. Slide a dark-colored 8mm bead
on the wire to the end wraps. Then
slide a 3mm bead onto the wire.
Continue to slide beads randomly
onto the wire, alternating each larger
bead with a 3mm bead.

When 18" of the wire is filled with
beads, wrap the beaded portion of
the wire around the paper towel tube,
spiraling the wire. Slip the wire off
the roll. Shape the wire to widen the
bottom spiral for the base of the tree.
Continue to slide beads onto the wire
in the same manner, stopping 6" from
the end and using only 3mm beads
for the last ³/₄". Shape the upper
beaded portion of the wire into
smaller and smaller spirals to resemble
a tree shape. Slip a 4mm bead, the
filigree cap, and a final fancy bead
onto the wire. Wrap the wire three
times around the tip of the needle-
nose pliers above the final bead.
Cut off the excess wire with the wire
cutters. Flatten the cut end.♥

Ribbon Topiary Tree
Shown on page 11.

YOU WILL NEED

5" to 6"-tall silverplate bowl
3"-diameter Styrofoam ball or cube
Crafts knife
1¹/₂" square of thick double-stick adhesive
Tissue paper: white and silver

8" length of ⁵/₁₆"-diameter wooden dowel
Mod Podge decoupage medium
1"-wide foam brush
12 to 15 natural or black velvet leaves
1¹/₁₆" straight pins
12"-tall Styrofoam cone
1½"-wide wire-edge ribbon: 4¼ yards
   of gold wire mesh and 3¾ yards each
   of gold luster and gold sparkle
Tacky glue
3½"-tall plastic gold snowflake
Sewing thread and needle
2 to 3 bronze berry sprays

INSTRUCTIONS
Use the crafts knife to trim the
Styrofoam ball or cube to fit inside
the bowl. Attach the ball to the bowl
with double-stick adhesive. Stuff
crumpled pieces of white tissue paper
in the space between the bowl and
the ball to prevent the ball from
moving. Apply glue to one end of the
dowel and insert the dowel into the
center of the ball for the tree trunk.
Use Mod Podge to glue a strip of silver
tissue paper around the bottom 2" of
the tree trunk. Use straight pins to
attach the velvet leaves around the
base of the tree trunk, overlapping
the leaves and covering the ball.

For the tree, use Mod Podge to glue
strips of silver tissue paper over the
Styrofoam cone. Let the tree dry. Insert
the remaining end of the dowel into
the center bottom of the tree until the
tissue paper reaches the bottom of
the cone. Temporarily remove the
tree from the dowel.
   Cut three 45" lengths from each of
the wire-edge ribbons. Set aside the
remaining gold wire mesh ribbon.
Working with a length of gold luster
ribbon, pull the wire at one edge so
the ribbon begins to gather. Fold the
ribbon end over itself two times; glue
in place. Pull the opposite end of the
same wire, gathering the ribbon to
measure 20". Fold this ribbon end over
itself two times and glue in place. Trim
the wire. Repeat for each ribbon length.
   Pin the gathered edge of one gold
luster ribbon length to the tree,
beginning 1" from the bottom of the
cone and spacing the pins 1" apart.
Encircle the tree with the gold luster
ribbon one time and then spiral the
ribbon upwards. Next pin the gathered
edge of the one mesh ribbon length to
the tree, overlapping the ribbon ends
¼". Then pin a gold sparkle ribbon
length around the tree. Repeat with
ribbon lengths, alternating the ribbons
in the same order.
   Dab some glue on the dowel above
the tissue paper. Place the tree on the
dowel. Glue the snowflake to the top
of the tree. Remove the wire from one
edge of the reserved mesh ribbon.
Sew together the ends of the ribbon,
forming a circle. Hand-sew running
stitches along the edge of the ribbon
without wire. Slip the ribbon circle
over the snowflake. Pull the thread
ends so the ribbon gathers as tight
as possible around the base of the
snowflake. Knot the thread. Pin the
gathered edge of the ribbon to the
top of the tree.
   Pull apart the berry sprays. Glue
individual berries between the ruffled
ribbon layers.♥

Fancy Button Card Ornament
Shown above.

YOU WILL NEED
8½×11" sheet of gold parchment paper
Fiskars Corner Rounder
2¾×4⅞" piece each of blush card stock
   and marbleized paper
Glue stick
Buttonhole twist or carpet thread
2 or 3 fancy buttons
Tacky glue
Deckle-edge scissors
6" length of fine gold or silver cord
9" length of narrow gold or silver
   twisted cord

INSTRUCTIONS
Photocopy the button card label pattern
on *page 20* onto gold parchment
paper. Trim the label to measure
2½×4⅛". Round the corners with the
Corner Rounder. Center and glue the
label onto the lower portion of the
card stock. Referring to the pattern

for placement, use buttonhole twist or carpet thread to sew the buttons onto the label. Apply glue to the knots and thread ends at the back of the card stock. Glue the marbleized paper to the back of the card stock. Trim the top and bottom edges of the button card with deckle-edge scissors. For the hanger, use a needle threaded with fine cord to sew through the top center of the card; knot the cord ends together. Tie the narrow twisted cord into a bow; glue the bow to the base of the hanger on the card front.♥

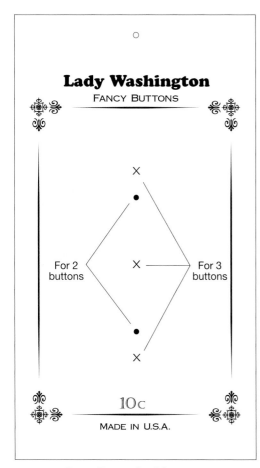

Fancy Button Card Ornament

Vintage Flower Wreath
Shown on page 12.

YOU WILL NEED
15" artificial pine wreath
Vintage flowers: mauve rose, peach rose, lavender cluster, 3 lilac sprays, 2 columbine sprays, 3 wild rose sprays, 3 freesia sprays, and 5 berry clusters
Cloth-covered 32-gauge floral wire
Old, ivory glove
Velvet leaf stems: 9 beige ombre and 5 shell pink ombre
Mod Podge decoupage medium
1"-wide foam brush
Glitter: gold and mauve
8—1"-diameter silver glass bulbs
3 bronze berry clusters
7 bronze berry sprays
3 pieces of old or broken jewelry
Platinum bullion
Old photograph

INSTRUCTIONS
Arrange the vintage flowers around the wreath, placing the most dramatic flower at the center top of the wreath. When pleased with the arrangement, wire the flower stems to the wreath. Wrap a length of floral wire around the glove below the palm. Attach the glove wire near the center bottom of the wreath.

Lightly brush Mod Podge onto the velvet leaf stems in an uneven fashion. Immediately pour gold or mauve glitter onto the wet surface, tap off the excess glitter, and set the leaves aside to dry. Lightly brush Mod Podge onto the top of a few of the glass bulbs. Immediately pour glitter onto the wet surface, tap off the excess glitter, and set the bulbs aside to dry.

Arrange the berry clusters and sprays around the wreath. When pleased with the arrangement, wire the clusters and sprays in place. Arrange and wire the glittered leaf stems and bulbs among the flowers and berries. Wire the jewelry pieces to the wreath. Stretch and wire the platinum bullion around the wreath. Wire the photo to the wreath.♥

Compact Ornament
Shown below.

YOU WILL NEED
2—2¹⁄₂"-diameter button cover forms
Wire cutters
2—4" squares of dusty peach velvet
2 purchased fancy beaded appliqué trims, about 2¹⁄₄"-diameter
Tacky glue
¹⁄₄ yard of ¹⁄₂"-wide gold or silver metallic trim
5" length of ¹⁄₈"-wide gold or silver metallic trim

INSTRUCTIONS
Use wire cutters to remove the metal shank from the back of each button cover form. Cover the button cover forms with velvet following the manufacturer's instructions. Glue a beaded appliqué trim on the front of each form. Glue the ¹⁄₂"-wide trim to the back edge of one of the forms. For the hanging loop, fold the 5" length of ¹⁄₈"-wide trim in half. Glue the ends to the top center back of the same form. Squeeze a bead of glue along the back edge of the remaining form. Let the glue set for 30 seconds. Press the backs of the forms together until they adhere to each other. Let the glue dry completely.♥

Photograph Ornament
Shown at right.

YOU WILL NEED
Card stock: 8½×11" sheet each of ivory marbled and sepia-toned
Straight-edge
Bone folder
Glue stick or double-stick tape
Deckle-edge scissors
Marbled paper: magenta and mauve
Small old photograph
4—¼"–½"-wide fancy ribbon trims, including a 15" length of ½"-wide ribbon trim for the hanging loop
Fancy button or piece of jewelry
Sewing thread and needle
Transparent tape
Crafts knife

INSTRUCTIONS
Cut a 3½×11" piece of ivory marbled card stock for the base. Referring to the diagram *below*, use the bone folder to score the card stock 4½" and 9" from one short edge. Trim the 2" area below the last score line into a point, rounding the end for the tab. Fold the base on the scored lines.

For the layered front papers, cut a 3×4" rectangle from the remaining ivory marbled card stock. Mount the ivory rectangle on the sepia-toned card stock with a glue stick or double-stick tape. Use the deckle-edge scissors to cut around the ivory card stock, creating a ⅛" sepia-toned border. Mount the sepia-toned card stock on the magenta marbled paper. Cut a ⅛" magenta marbled paper border with the deckle-edge scissors.

Trim the photograph to measure about 1¾×2⅝". To make the arch, trace around the lid or circle template at the top back of the photo. Cut on the traced line. Mount the photo on sepia-toned card stock. Use the deckle-edge scissors to cut around the photo, creating a ⅛" sepia-toned border.

Referring to the photograph *above right*, mount the layered photo and the ribbon trims on the layered front papers. Use a needle and thread to sew the button to the bottom right corner of the layered papers.

For the hanger, fold the 15" length of ribbon trim in half, crossing the ribbon at the center of the base front. Secure the ribbon to the base with transparent tape. Mount the layered front paper on the base front over the ribbon hanger.

To add stability, cut a 3×4" rectangle of sepia-toned card stock and a 3×4" rectangle of mauve marbled paper. Mount the sepia-toned rectangle on the inside surface of the base back and the mauve rectangle on the outside surface of the base back. Use the crafts knife to cut a 1½"-long slit in the base back about 1¼" from the bottom edge. Insert the tab into the slit to form a tent shape. ♥

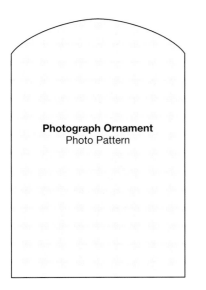

Photograph Ornament
Photo Pattern

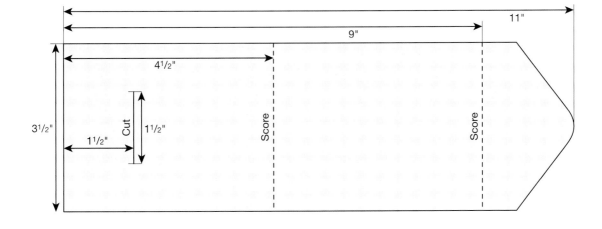

Victorian Splendor

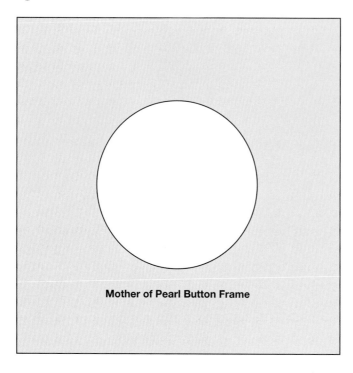

Mother of Pearl Button Frame

Mother of Pearl Button Frame
Shown above.

YOU WILL NEED
2—3$\frac{1}{2}$" squares of mat board
Crafts knife
3$\frac{1}{2}$" square of batting
Tacky glue
3"-wide disposable paint roller
5" square of dusty peach velvet
5×10" rectangle of gold crinkle fabric
12" length of $\frac{1}{2}$"-wide metallic gold trim
5" length of $\frac{1}{8}$"-wide metallic gold trim
20 to 25 assorted mother-of-pearl buttons
1 fancy button or piece of jewelry
Glue gun and hotmelt adhesive
E-6000 adhesive

INSTRUCTIONS
Using the pattern *above,* trace the circle onto one mat board square. Use a crafts knife to cut out the circle for the frame opening. Center and glue the batting on the frame front with glue. Trim the batting even with the outer edges and with the frame opening edges. Center the velvet over the batting. Flip the frame front over and snugly wrap the velvet edges around to the back of the frame, trimming away excess at the corners. Glue the edges in place.

Cut one 5" and one 3" square of crinkle fabric. Use the roller to apply a coat of glue to one side of the remaining mat board square. Center the 5" square of crinkle fabric over the wet glue. Smooth the fabric to the board and wrap the edges around to the back of the mat board square; glue in place. Glue the 3" fabric square to the uncovered side of the mat board square, covering the wrapped fabric edges. This is the wrong side of the frame back.

Glue the $\frac{1}{2}$"-wide trim to three edges on the wrong side of the frame back. For the hanger, fold the $\frac{1}{8}$"-wide trim in half, forming a loop. Glue the trim ends to the top center on the wrong side of the frame back. With right sides facing out, hot glue the frame front to the back along the three trimmed edges.

Arrange and glue the buttons to the frame front with E-6000 adhesive.♥

Village Houses
Shown below and on page 7.

YOU WILL NEED
Variety of house drawings
Colored pencils
Spray adhesive
Foam-core board
Crafts knife
Small boxes
Glue or tape

INSTRUCTIONS
Using a copy machine, enlarge the house drawings on a copy machine to the desired sizes. Color the houses with colored pencils. Roughly trim the excess paper away from the houses, cutting a straight edge along the bottom of each house. Apply spray adhesive to the back of the colored houses. Press the houses, adhesive side down, onto foam core board, positioning the bottom of the house along an outer edge of the foam core. Use the crafts knife to cut out each house. Center and glue or tape a small box to the bottom back edge of each foam-core mounted house.♥

Beaded Tassel Ornament
Shown at near right.

YOU WILL NEED
Wooden pieces: 1⅛" candle cup,
    20mm round bead, and 1" length
    of ⅜"-diameter dowel
Metallic gold acrylic paint
Paintbrush
Tacky glue
Miniature silver glass marbles
Mod Podge decoupage medium
⅓ yard of 3"-wide gold beaded fringe
6" length of 1"-wide amber beaded fringe
Gold stranded seed beads
6" length of ⅛"-wide metallic gold trim

INSTRUCTIONS
Paint the candle cup and round bead metallic gold; let the paint dry. Cover the top half of the round bead with glue. Immediately pour the miniature silver marbles onto the wet glue; press the marbles into the glue. When dry, coat the beaded area with Mod Podge. Set aside to dry.

Beginning at one end of the dowel, wrap and glue the 3"-wide fringe around the dowel. Gradually spiral the fringe upwards toward the opposite end. Wrap and glue the 1"-wide fringe around the top end of the dowel. Let the tassel dry.

Glue the stranded seed beads around the candle cup. When dry, glue the top of the dowel into the candle cup.

For the hanging loop, fold the ⅛"-wide trim in half, forming a loop; knot together the trim ends. Slip the loop through the round bead hole. Glue the knot inside the hole. Glue the bottom of the round bead to the top of the candle cup.♥

Fringe Tassel Ornament
Shown above right.

YOU WILL NEED
1¹⁄₁₆" finial dowel cap
Metallic gold acrylic paint
Paintbrush
1"-diameter clear glass or
    mother-of-pearl button
Tacky glue
4" length of 4mm pearl trim
18" length each of 5"-wide ivory and gold
    rayon French twist knot fringe
Glue gun and hotmelt adhesive
1 yard of narrow gold cording
Length of 2"-wide tassel fringe needed
    for 4 small tassels
6" length of ⅛"-wide gold metallic trim
5" length each of 1"-wide ivory chenille
    looped fringe and 1"-wide gold
    metallic fringe

INSTRUCTIONS
Paint the finial dowel cap metallic gold. When the paint is dry, glue the button to the top of the cap with tacky glue. When the glue is dry, glue the pearl trim around the edge of the button. Set aside to dry.

Hot-glue the finished edges of the 5"-wide fringes together, tightly rolling the edges while gluing.

Cut the narrow gold cording into four 9" lengths. Slip one length of cord through the top of a small tassel and tie the cording together just above the tassel. Repeat for each small tassel. Evenly spacing the tassels, glue the cording ends to the top outer edge of the rolled fringe so the tassels hang flush with the bottom of the fringe.

For the hanging loop, insert the ends of the ⅛"-wide trim through the buttonholes and then through the cap; knot the trim ends together. Pull the trim so the knot rests against the inside of the cap; glue the knot in place.

Glue the top of the rolled fringe to the bottom edge of the cap. Glue the 1"-wide ivory chenille fringe around the space between the cap and the top of the rolled fringe. Glue the 1"-wide metallic fringe above the chenille fringe.♥

Gifts of the Magi

Sometimes the reason for the season gets lost in all the preparations, parties, and purchases. To keep the meaning of Christmas close to your heart, create a tree that tells the story, *opposite*. This one underscores the Magi with adornments so rich and regal you can almost catch the aroma of frankincense and myrrh. The crown topper, *above*, cascading swaddles of sheer fabric, dozens of ornaments, and Nativity collections pay homage to the long journey to Bethlehem on that special starry night. Instructions begin on *page 30*.

Commemorate the beauty and mystery of the first Christmas with this star-studded wreath of greens and handcrafted finery, *above*. Adorned in 3- and 5-inch papier-mâché stars—some covered in fabric, others scattered with glitter—the pine "halo" sweetly heralds the season suspended from a vintage-style horn. Beads, buttons, and metallic braid set it shimmering.

More than a gift holder, more than a pretty mantel decoration, a stocking that's lovingly crafted embodies all the warmth and sentimentality of the season. Resplendent in silk brocade and damask, one of these majestic stockings, *opposite*, may be the perfect gift to stitch for someone you love. Notice the coin and bead fringes on the cuffs: They softly jingle each time a treasure is slipped inside.

Invite the kids to lend a hand and make this Nativity scene, *above*, a family affair. Created from lengths of turned and gold-burnished wood, each figure shines with its own personality when plain and fancy ribbons are glued and belted in place. (See *page 40* for the instructions.)

Crafters will appreciate the sheer brilliance of this ornamental quintet, *opposite*. Assembled like decorated cookies, the Magi, elephant, and camel designs are quick to cut out with cookie cutters. Just press the cutters into a sheet of modeling compound rolled $1/4$-inch thick. Sprinkle the cutouts with beads for "icing" and pop them into the oven. Once they've cooled completely, string them to the tree.

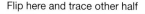

Gifts of the Magi

Crown Tree Topper
Shown on page 25.

YOU WILL NEED
Tracing paper
¼ yard of purple-and-gold brocade fabric
2—6"-diameter Styrofoam disks
15×20" piece of poster board
Industrial-strength adhesive
7" to 9"-tall papier-mâché cone
20×30" sheet of gold metallic paper
Tacky glue
Foam paint brush
Polyester fiberfill
3½ yards of ⅜"-wide gold metallic trim
2½ yards of ½"-wide gold metallic trim
24-gauge gold wire
Wire cutters
5—1⅛"-diameter gold jeweled buttons
8—⅝"-diameter gold buttons
2" gold filigree piece
12"-wide wire-edged sheer ribbon:
   1½ yards of copper and 3 yards of gold

INSTRUCTIONS
Trace the patterns, *opposite* and *left,* onto tracing paper. Cut out the pattern pieces. Use the pattern pieces to cut two front/backs and two sides from the brocade fabric. Sew all pieces with right sides together, using a ¼" seam allowance unless otherwise noted.

Sew one side piece to each side edge of a front/back piece, stopping at the dots as indicated on the pattern. Sew the other front/back piece to the remaining edges of each of the sides. Press the seam allowances open.

Trace around a Styrofoam disk on a piece of poster board; cut out the circle and set it aside. For the crown base, glue the two Styrofoam disks together with industrial-strength adhesive. When the glue has dried, use a hand-drilling motion to work the tip of the papier-mâché cone through the center of the base until the tip protrudes 2" above the top disk. Remove the cone from the hole; cut off 1" from the tip. Use glue and a foam brush to cover the cone with gold metallic paper. Glue the paper-covered cone into the hole in the base.

Pad the top of the base with polyester fiberfill. Squeeze a small amount of glue into the cone tip. Slip the fabric crown over the fiberfill and the base. Push the fabric center into the glue in the cone tip; let the glue dry. Add more fiberfill if needed. Glue the bottom edge of the fabric to the bottom edge of the base.

Cut two 18" lengths of ⅜"-wide gold metallic trim. Weave 24-gauge gold wire in and out of each length to stiffen the trim; cut the wire ends even with the trim. Shape one length over the top of the crown. Glue the center of the trim to the center top of the crown and glue the ends to the bottom edge of the base, following the seams. Repeat with the second length of wire.

Trace the fancy crown trim pattern onto poster board one time and onto gold metallic paper two times. Cut out the poster board shape on the traced line. Cut out one gold paper shape ½" outside the traced line and the second paper shape just inside the traced line. Glue the larger gold paper shape to the front of the poster board shape; wrap the excess paper around the edges to the back side, trimming as necessary. Glue the smaller paper shape to the back of the poster board shape.

To decorate the fancy crown trim, glue the ½"-wide gold metallic trim to the bottom edge and the ⅜"-wide trim along all the remaining edges. Glue a button below each crown point, alternating three large buttons with small buttons for the front of the crown. Wrap the fancy crown trim around the crown, aligning the bottom edges; glue in place.

Draw and cut out a 2"-diameter circular opening in the center of the set-aside circle of poster board. Cut a slash from the outer edge to the center opening. Cover one side of the poster board circle with gold

Crown Tree Topper
Fancy Crown Trim
Cut 1 from cardboard

Extend
to 1¼"

30

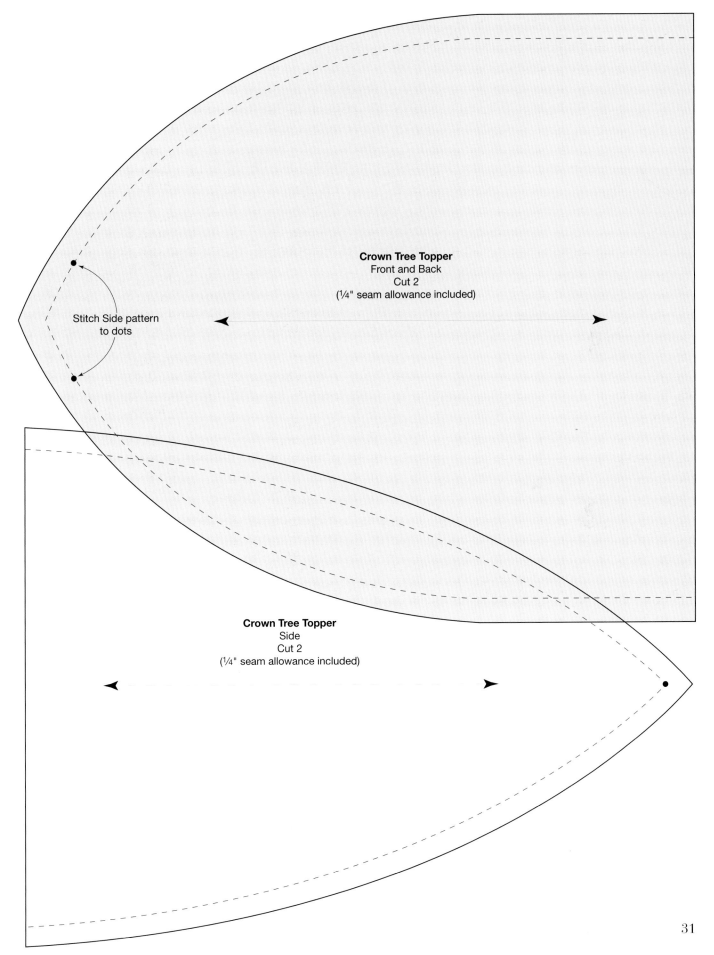

Crown Tree Topper
Front and Back
Cut 2
(¼" seam allowance included)

Stitch Side pattern
to dots

Crown Tree Topper
Side
Cut 2
(¼" seam allowance included)

31

metallic paper, wrapping the excess paper over the edges to the back at the outer and inner edges. Glue the paper-covered circle to the bottom of the crown, bending it to fit around the cone. Glue ½"-wide trim to the bottom of the base, positioning it around the outer edge and around the center opening edge.

Cut the shanks off the remaining large buttons. Glue a button to each side of the filigree piece. Glue the filigree to the center top of the crown.

To add fabric around the crown, pull the wire on one edge of the 12"-wide ribbon to gather the length. Wrap the gold ribbon around the cone just below the crown, securing it with the wire; trim off the excess wire. Then wrap the copper ribbon around the cone over the gold ribbon in the same manner.♥

Designed by Mary Jo Hiney

Star Wreath
Shown above and on page 26.

YOU WILL NEED
22"-diameter artificial pine wreath
Papier-mâché stars: 8—3", and 7—5"
Darning needle
26-gauge wire: dark green and gold
Wire cutters
Needle-nose pliers
Metallic gold acrylic paint
2—1"-wide foam brushes
Brocade fabrics: purple, red, green, orange, and fuchsia
Tacky glue
8—⅝" to 1⅛"-diameter jeweled buttons
Glue gun and hotmelt adhesive
Glitter: royal blue, magenta, turquoise, red, and periwinkle
Paper plates
Mod Podge decoupage medium
9-foot-long jewel-toned bead garland
5—2½" frosted glass ornaments
Assorted specialty beads in turquoise, royal blue, and magenta
1 yard each of gold/ dusty green and gold/dusty cinnamon 1"-wide metallic braid

INSTRUCTIONS
Use the darning needle to puncture two holes at the center back of each star. Cut fifteen 7" lengths of dark green wire. Insert a wire length through the holes on the back of each star. Use the needle-nose pliers to twist the wire ends tightly together next to the star. Using a foam brush, paint the back of each star with metallic gold. Let the paint dry.

To cover a star with fabric, cut a piece of brocade 1" larger than the width of the star. Use the glue. Apply glue to the front of the star with a foam brush. Center the fabric piece over the glue and wrap the excess fabric around the points to the opposite side, trimming the fabric as necessary. Dab glue on the fabric at the star tips and smooth the edges on the back. For our wreath, three of the small stars and five of the large stars are covered with fabric.

Remove the shanks from the jeweled buttons. Hot-glue a button to the center front of each fabric-covered star. Apply glue to the front of each star. Working over a paper plate, immediately pour one color of glitter over the wet glue; tap off the excess glitter. Set the star aside. When the glue is dry, apply a coat of Mod Podge to the glitter. Immediately sprinkle the star a second time with glitter. Let the Mod Podge dry.

To add beads, cut an 8" length of gold wire. Slip an end of a gold wire through the dark green wire at the back of a glittered star. Twist the gold

wire to the dark green wire to secure. Drape the gold wire across the star front and slide on several specialty beads. Bring the wire to the back of the star and twist the remaining end to the dark green wire; trim off the excess gold wire. Repeat for each glittered star.

Drape the bead garland around the wreath and secure it with the dark green wire. Arrange the stars and frosted ornaments on the wreath, referring to the photograph on *page 26*. When pleased with the arrangement, wire the stars and ornaments to the wreath. Tie an off-center bow with each length of braid. Position the bows on the wreath and secure with dark green wire. Weave the braid ends around the wreath.

For a hanging loop, fold a piece of dark green wire in half. Secure the ends to the top center back of wreath.♥

Designed by Mary Jo Hiney

Silk Brocade Stocking
Shown on page 27.

YOU WILL NEED
For one stocking:
Graph paper
⅝ yard of traditional silk brocade
¼ yard of contrasting fabric for cuff
Matching sewing thread
½ yard of 1½"-wide beaded fringe trim
¼ yard of gold coin fringe

INSTRUCTIONS
Enlarge the stocking pattern, *page 15*, and cuff pattern, *opposite*, onto graph paper. Cut out the pattern pieces. Sew all pieces with right sides together, using ¼" seam allowances unless otherwise noted.

Cut the Fabrics
Cut two stockings from the silk brocade for the stocking front and back. From the contrasting fabric, cut two cuff pieces for the cuff and the cuff lining, and a 2×5" strip for the hanging loop.

Sew the Stockings

Sew the stocking front to the back, leaving the top edge open. Clip the curves. Press the seam allowances open as much as possible. Press the remaining seam allowances toward the stocking back. Turn the stocking right side out.

For the hanging loop, press the long edges of the 2×5" strip under ¼". Fold the strip in half lengthwise, aligning the pressed edges; press again. Sew the long edges together opposite the fold. Fold the strip in half, forming the loop. Baste the ends to the top inside corner on the heel side of the stocking with the loop inside the stocking.

For the cuff, sew the short edges together with a ½" seam allowance, forming a circle. Press the seam allowances open. Repeat with the cuff lining. Pin the beaded fringe trim to the bottom edge of the cuff, aligning raw edges. Use a zipper foot to baste the trim to the cuff as close to the beads as possible. With right sides together and using a zipper foot, sew the bottom edges of the cuff and the cuff lining together along the basting line. Turn the cuff right side out; press.

Slip the cuff inside the stocking with the right side of the cuff facing the wrong side of the stocking. Sew the top edges together with a ½" seam allowance. Pull the cuff away from the stocking and press the seam allowances toward the stocking. Edge-stitch around the stocking opening by sewing ¼" from the top of the stocking, through the stocking and seam allowance layers.

Turn under the ends of the coin fringe tape. Hand-sew the ends to the front of the cuff about ½" below the top edge so the fringe drapes slightly.♥

Designed by Mary Jo Hiney

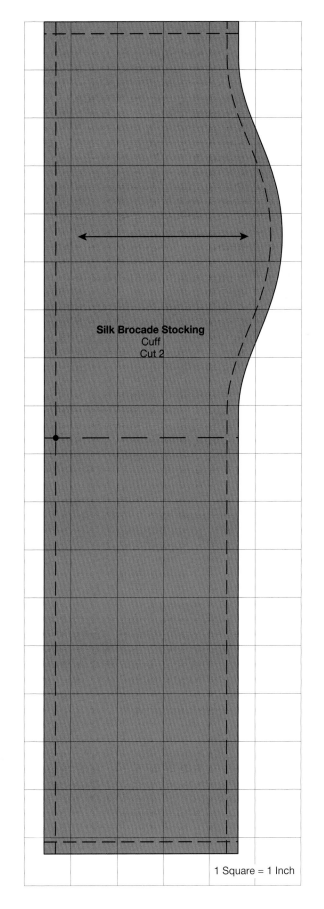

Silk Brocade Stocking
Cuff
Cut 2

1 Square = 1 Inch

Papier-Mâché Star Ornament
Shown above left.

YOU WILL NEED
For one ornament:
7" papier-mâché double-sided star
8" square of brightly colored fabric
3"-wide disposable paint roller
Tacky glue
5" square of gold metallic paper
9" length of fine gold cording for the
    hanging loop
Sewing needle
Assorted gold metallic trims and fancy
    braids, $1/2$" to $5/8$"-wide
$5/8$"-diameter gold-jeweled button
6"-diameter round paper doily
Krylon Short Cuts paint pen: Gold Leaf
$1/4$ yard of gold coin fringe

INSTRUCTIONS
Use the glue and the paint roller to
attach the fabric to the papier-mâché
star. Center the brightly colored fabric
on one side of the star and wrap the
excess fabric around the points on
the opposite side, trimming the fabric
as necessary. For the center back of
the star, cut the gold metallic paper
into a pentagon shape large enough
to cover the edges of the fabric; glue
the paper to the back.

For the hanging loop, thread a
needle with fine gold cording and
pull it through the center top of the
star; knot the cording ends together.

To decorate the star, refer to the
photograph *above*. Drape and glue
the gold metallic trims and fancy braids
on the star. Glue the gold-jeweled
button to the center front of the star.
Color the doily with the Gold Leaf
paint pen. Cut pieces of doily to wrap
around the two bottom points of the
star; glue them in place.

Cut the gold coin fringe into four
lengths of 3 or 4 coins. Apply glue to
all the cut edges to prevent fraying.
When the glue is dry, fold under the
ends to meet at the center back of
each length. Hand-sew running stitches
through the tape, pull the thread
tightly, and knot to secure. Glue the
coins to the top three points of the
star and to the center back.♥
Designed by Mary Jo Hiney

Vellum Star Ornament
Shown above right.

YOU WILL NEED
For one ornament:
Tracing paper
$1^1/2$ sheets of $8^1/2 \times 11$" vellum in color of
    your choice

Krylon Short Cuts paint pen: Gold Leaf
Ultra fine-tip gold paint pen
Sewing needle
Sewing thread to match the paper
9" length of narrow gold cord
Mod Podge decoupage medium
Fine gold glitter

INSTRUCTIONS
Trace the vellum star pattern, *opposite,*
onto tracing paper, including the
center design. Cut out the pattern.
Trace six stars onto the vellum; cut
the shapes along the lines.

Place a vellum star over the pattern
and use the Gold Leaf paint pen to
draw the center star on one side of
the vellum, drawing directly over the
traced lines. Also, draw along the
outer edges of the star with the Gold
Leaf paint pen. Randomly add dots
around the center design with the
ultra fine-tip gold paint pen. When the
gold leaf and paint are dry, turn the
star over and make a mirror image of
the design on the opposite side.
Repeat for each vellum star.

Fold each star in half and crease.
Align the six stars. Use the sewing
needle to make punctures through
the layered stars, spacing the punctures
about $3/8$" apart along the center fold.
Sew the stars together through the
punctures with a doubled thread,
securing the thread with a knot at each
end of the star.

For the hanging cord, thread the fine
gold cord through the top puncture;
knot the cord ends together.

To add glitter, squeeze the star layers
together between your thumb and
forefinger. Use your other forefinger
to apply Mod Podge the top edges
of the layered stars. Immediately
sprinkle fine gold glitter over the wet
Mod Podge. Fan out the star layers
and let the Mod Podge dry.♥
Designed by Mary Jo Hiney

Base
Cut 1 from brass foil

Star
Cut 1 from copper foil

Gold Tassel Ornament

Vellum Star Ornament
Cut 6 for each star

Fold

Gold Tassel Ornament
Shown below.

YOU WILL NEED
Tracing paper
36-gauge brass and copper tooling foil
Ballpoint pen
Tape
Small, sharp manicure scissors
Triangle hole punch
Scribbles 3-D Paint: Glittering Gold
Miniature gold glass marbles
Small bowl
Goop adhesive
Jewel-tone glass nugget
3"-long gold tassel
10" length of gold cord

INSTRUCTIONS
Trace the ornament patterns, *above,* onto tracing paper. Unroll the brass and copper foil. Lay the traced base pattern over the brass foil and the star pattern over the copper foil; tape them in place. Use a ballpoint pen to firmly emboss the designs onto the foils, drawing directly over the traced lines. Carefully remove the pattern. Cut out the foil shapes with manicure scissors. Use the triangle hole punch to make a hole in each corner of the base.

Apply a thin line of the Glittering Gold paint to the front edges of the base. Immediately sprinkle the gold glass marbles onto the paint over a small bowl. Let the paint dry.

Use Goop adhesive to glue the copper star to the center of the brass base and the glass nugget to the center of the star. Glue the tassel to the bottom of the ornament.

For the hanging loop, insert the gold cord through the bottom hole; knot the cord ends together.♥

Designed by Kristin Detrick

Coin Pouch Ornament
Shown on page 36.

YOU WILL NEED
For one ornament:
Tracing paper
7×18" rectangle of silk shimmer organza
Matching sewing thread
18" length of narrow gold twisted cord
Fabric stiffener
Gold coins

INSTRUCTIONS
Trace the pattern, on *page 36,* onto tracing paper. Cut out the pattern. Use the pattern to cut two pouches from the organza.

With right sides facing and using a ¼" seam allowance, sew the pouches together along the side and bottom edges, leaving the top edge open and

a ½" opening on one side as indicated on the pattern. Finger-press the seam allowances open.

To form the casing, press under 1" at the top edge of the pouch. Sew through both layers of fabric ⅜" and ¾" from the pressed edge. Thread the narrow twisted cord through the casing of the pouch. Knot the cording ends together.

Dip the pouch in fabric stiffener. Ring out excess stiffener and shape the pouch. Let the pouch dry overnight. Fill the bag with gold coins. ♥

Designed by Mary Jo Hiney

Crown Ornament
Shown below.

YOU WILL NEED

For one ornament:
2½"-diameter Styrofoam ball
Sharp kitchen knife
Jewel-toned tissue paper
Foam brush
Mod Podge decoupage medium
2—6½" lengths of ⅝"-wide fancy ribbon
Large safety pin
2" eye pin
Silver-lined rochaille glass bead
Smooth gold sequin
Etched gold bead
Scribbles 3-D Paint: Glittering Gold
Tracing paper
36-gauge brass tooling foil
Ballpoint pen
Small, sharp manicure scissors
Miniature gold glass marbles
Small bowl
3—5mm round faceted acrylic stones
Glue gun and hotmelt adhesive
8½" length of 3/16"-diameter gold twisted cording
9" length of fine gold cord

INSTRUCTIONS

Use a sharp kitchen knife to cut ½" from the bottom of the Styrofoam ball. Cut 1" squares of tissue paper. Apply Mod Podge to about one-fourth of the ball with a foam brush. Smooth one piece of tissue at a time onto the wet area of the ball. Apply a coat of Mod Podge over the tissue. Repeat to cover the entire ball, including the

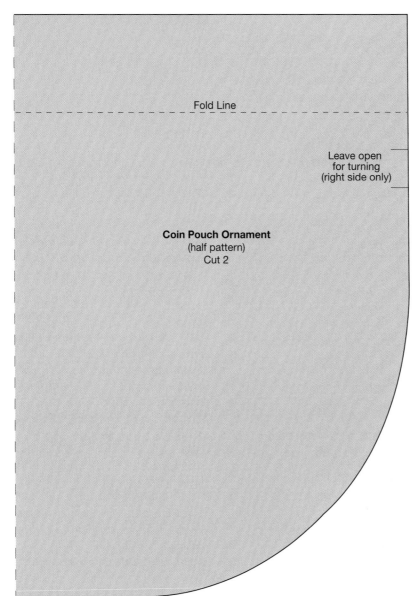

Fold Line

Leave open
for turning
(right side only)

Coin Pouch Ornament
(half pattern)
Cut 2

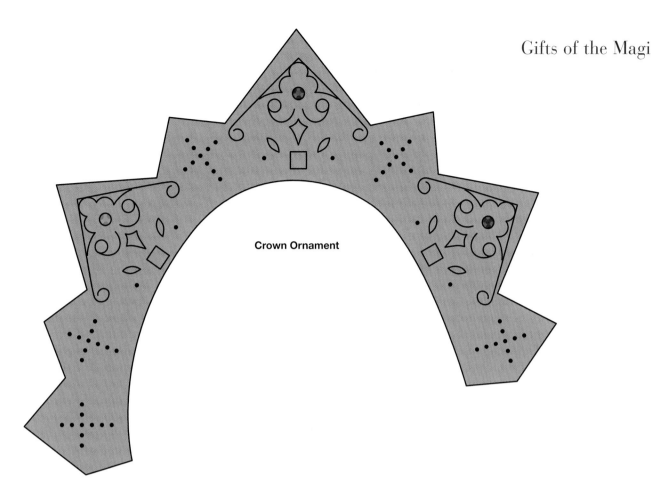

Crown Ornament

bottom. Apply as many layers of tissue as desired. Immediately apply Mod Podge to the wrong side of the fancy ribbon length. Press the ribbon lengths over the top of the ball, crossing the ribbons at the center top. Let the ball dry for 24 hours.

Use the large safety pin to make a hole down into the ball at the center top. Place the rochaille bead, gold sequin, and gold etched bead on the eye pin. Insert the beaded eye pin in the hole and glue in place with the Glittering Gold paint.

Trace the pattern *above* onto tracing paper. Unroll the brass foil. Lay the traced pattern over the foil and tape in place. Use the ballpoint pen to firmly emboss the design onto the foil, drawing directly over the traced lines. Remove the pattern. Cut out the foil shape with manicure scissors.

Apply a thin line of the Glittering Gold paint to the front edges of the foil shape. Immediately sprinkle the gold glass marbles onto the paint over a small bowl. Use the paint to glue the faceted stones to the front of the

foil shape as indicated on the pattern. Let the paint dry.

Bend the foil shape around the bottom of the ball, trimming the foil to overlap ¼" at the center back of the crown. Beginning at the center front, hot-glue the bottom edge of the foil to the ball. Hot-glue the gold twisted cording to the bottom edge of the crown.

For the hanging loop, thread the fine gold cord through the top of the eye pin; knot the cord ends together.♥
Designed by Kristin Detrick

Glass Nugget Ornaments
Shown on page 38.

YOU WILL NEED
3mm-thick glass oval shape with
    predrilled hole
Glass nuggets in assorted colors,
    approximately 12 per ornament
Elmer's clear silicone sealant
Newspaper
Drinking straw
Disposable rubber gloves
Non-sanded tile grout: charcoal

Old bowl and spoon
Sponge
Clear satin-finish spray sealer
10" length of gold cord
12" length of 1"-wide sheer ribbon

INSTRUCTIONS
Arrange approximately 12 assorted glass nuggets on the glass oval. Use silicone sealant to glue the nuggets to the oval; let the glue set overnight.

Cover your work area with newspaper. To keep the hole clean, insert a 2" length of straw into the hole at the top of the ornament. Wearing disposable gloves, mix the grout in an old bowl according to the instructions on the grout package. When the grout is the consistency of peanut butter, spread it onto the ornament.

Check the grout after 1 hour. If the grout is not semi-hard, continue to check it every hour until it reaches the correct consistency. When the grout is semi-hard, use a damp sponge to smooth the grout on the ornament surface and to wipe away the excess from the top of the nuggets. Carefully

remove the straw from the hole. If any grout breaks off, mix a new small batch of grout and repair the area. Let the grout dry overnight.

Spray the grout side of the ornament with clear satin finish sealer; let the finish dry. For the hanging loop, fold the cord in half and insert the fold through the hole. Bring the cord ends through the fold and pull the ends. Knot the cord ends together. Tie the ribbon into a bow around the base of the hanging loop.♥

Designed by Kristin Detrick

Beaded Clay Magi Ornaments
Shown on page 28.

YOU WILL NEED
Waxed paper
Sculpey III polymer clay: gold
Straight-sided drinking glass
Non-stick surface, such as a piece of
    poster board
Camel, 3 kings, and elephant cookie
    cutters (see Sources, *page 158*)
Tacky glue
Foam paintbrush
Toothpicks
Assorted bright shades and styles of
    beads, including seed, hex cut, bugle,
    round faceted, teardrops for the eyes,
    and fancy jewels for the kings' crowns
Miniature glass marbles
Beading needle
Sewing thread
Bent-nose tweezers

Aluminum foil
Baking sheet
Fine gold cording

INSTRUCTIONS
Cover your work area with a sheet of waxed paper. Knead the clay between the palms of your hands until it is soft and pliable. Place the clay on the shiny side of the poster board, and use a straight-sided drinking glass to roll out the clay until it is a scant ¼" thick. Lay the cookie cutters on the clay and trace around the shapes with a toothpick. Cut out the shapes with a knife.

Working with sections of one ornament at a time, use the foam paintbrush to spread a thin layer of glue over the front surface of the clay cutout. Stick a toothpick through the top center of the cutout to make a hole for the hanging loop.

Referring to the photo *below* or the illustrations *opposite* for ideas, decorate the cutouts with assorted beads. Detail the dominant design lines with the more dramatic beads, pressing them firmly into the glue-covered areas. To make a seed bead design line, string the beads on a threaded beading needle. Gently press the strung beads into the clay, carefully remove the thread, and then press them firmly into the clay. Use the bent-nose tweezers or the tip of a toothpick to position individual beads on the clay. Periodically lift the cutout from the work surface to prevent it from sticking.

When all the dominant design lines are beaded, add glue to the open areas, and press seed beads or miniature glass marbles into the spaces to completely cover them.

Place the ornaments on a baking sheet covered with aluminum foil. Put the baking sheet in the oven and bake the ornaments according to the instructions on the clay package.

When the ornaments are cool to the touch, thread a 9" length of narrow gold cording through the hole; knot the cording ends together.♥

Designed by Mary Jo Hiney

**Beaded Clay
Magi Ornaments**

Camel

King 1

King 2

King 3

Elephant

Nativity
Shown above, opposite, and on page 29.

YOU WILL NEED
For all pieces:
5-minute epoxy
18-gauge gold wire
Wire cutters and needle-nose pliers
Delta Renaissance Foil Gold Kit
Tacky glue
Variety of ribbons and trims in colors
   to match fabrics
$\frac{1}{4}$"-diameter gold cording
$\frac{1}{8}$"-diameter ivory cording

For the angel:
Wooden Shaker peg
Candleholder
Round wooden beads: 1 large for head and
   2 small for hands
$1\frac{1}{2}$"-wide ivory-and-gold ribbon
$\frac{1}{2}$ yard of ivory shimmery fabric
8" length of gold mini-string beads

For Baby Jesus and Cradle:
Wooden candle cup
Toy man
Scrap of gold shimmery fabric
2—6"-long wooden spindles
10" length of $2\frac{1}{2}$"-wide wire-edged ribbon

For each remaining figure:
1 wooden candlestick for body
Round wooden beads: 1 large for head and
   2 small for hands
$\frac{1}{2}$ yard of shimmery fabric for Mary,
   Joseph, and each king
$\frac{1}{2}$ yard of dull fabric for the shepherds
15" square of gold-and-ivory open weave
   fabric for Mary
1—$1\frac{1}{2}$"-diameter wheel for each crown
1 glass bead for each crown

For the gifts:
$1\frac{1}{2}$" wooden block
2 assorted wooden candleholders
2 round wooden beads to fit in the
   candleholders
2 small wooden finials
Scraps of fabric and ribbon
2 assorted glass beads

INSTRUCTIONS
Assemble the Pieces
Angel. Glue the shaker peg with epoxy into the candleholder and the large bead to the top of the shaker peg. For the wings, cut a 25" length of wire. Bend the wire to form a loop at the center and then shape a wing on either side of the loop. To attach

the wings, position them on one side of the peg and wrap a length of wire around the loop area and the peg to secure. For the arms, cut a 12" length of wire; wrap the center of the wire around the peg at shoulder height. Fold over $\frac{1}{4}$" at each end of the wire. Use the needle-nose pliers to pinch the folded area flat. Glue a bead hand to each wire end.

Baby Jesus. Glue the toy man with epoxy into the candle cup.

Remaining Figures. Glue the bead head with epoxy to the top of the candlestick. For the arms, cut a 12" length of wire for the taller figures and a 9" length for the shorter figures; wrap the center of the wire around the candlestick at "shoulder" height. Fold over $\frac{1}{4}$" at each end of the wire. Then use the needle-nose pliers to pinch the folded area flat. Glue a bead hand to each wire end.

Gifts. Glue a round bead with epoxy to the top of each candleholder and glue a finial to the top of one of the round beads. Set aside the remaining finial until later.

Apply the Foil
Following the instructions on the Delta Renaissance Foil Kit, apply paint, adhesive, and gold foil to the pieces. Finish the top 3" of each figure; the bottom 2" of the angel, including the base; all the bead hands; the wheels for the crowns; the spindles for the cradle; and the gifts, including the block and the finial set aside earlier.

Dress the Figures
Angel. Center a length of $1\frac{1}{2}$"-wide ivory-and-gold ribbon on the back of the peg; wrap it over the shoulders, and cross it in the front. Glue the ribbon ends to the peg. For the sleeves, center a 28" length of ribbon on the back of the peg, draping the ribbon over the wire. Wrap the ribbon

around each wire arm and bring the ribbon ends back to the peg; glue them in place.

For the skirt, measure from the arm wire to the bottom of the angel; double this measurement and add 4". Use this measurement to cut a square of ivory shimmery fabric. Fold the fabric in half and wrap the edge opposite the fold around the angel just below the arms; glue to secure. Glue ribbon or trim over the top edge of the skirt. For the hair, hold your thumb and forefinger 3" apart and wrap the ivory cording around your fingers five times. Remove 3 loops from your fingers and knot the ends together with an overhand knot. Glue the knot to the top of the head. Glue any stray loops to the head to lie flat. Glue short lengths of gold string beads in the hair.

Baby Jesus. Wrap the baby in gold shimmery fabric. Tie a ribbon around the center of the baby to secure the fabric. Cut a 1½" length of gold cording. Glue the cording ends to the center back of the head, for a halo.

Remaining Figures. For the skirt, measure from the arm wire to the bottom of the figure; double this measurement and add 1". Use this measurement to cut a square of shimmery or dull fabric. Set the skirt fabric aside.

From the length of the remaining fabric, cut two 2"-wide strips. For the sleeves, center one fabric strip on the back of the candlestick, draping the strip over the wire. Wrap the strip around each wire arm and bring the fabric ends back to the candlestick; glue the ends in place. To cover the chest, drape the remaining strip over the first, crossing the fabric over the front of the candlestick. Bring the ends to the back and cross them over the front again. Glue the ends to the candlestick.

Fold the skirt fabric in half and wrap the edge opposite the fold around the

figure just below the arms; glue to secure. Glue ribbon or trim over the top edge of the skirt, or tie cording around the waist for a belt.

Wrap long lengths of ribbon or fabric strips around the necks of the kings and Mary. To secure the fabric strips, wrap cording around the back of the neck, cross the cording in the front, and tie at the back.

For each king, cut a 12" square of shimmery fabric, rounding the corners. Fold under one corner of the fabric and glue to the top of the head. For the crown, glue the wheel to the fabric at the center top of the head. Glue trim, ribbon, or cording to the edges of the crown. Glue a glass bead to the center top of the crown.

For Mary's hair, hold your thumb and forefinger 4" apart and wrap the ivory cording around your fingers seven to eight times. Remove five loops from your fingers and knot the ends together with an overhand knot. Glue the knot to the top of the head and let the hair drape down the back. For the halo, cut a 2¼" length of gold cording. Glue the cording ends to the center back of the head, creating a circle. Cut the 15" square of open-weave fabric in half diagonally. Using one half, glue the center of the long edge to the back of the halo; drape the fabric ends over Mary's arms.

For Joseph and each of the shepherds, glue one end of gold cording to the center top of the head. Continue gluing the cording to the head working outward from the center in a clockwise direction. Cut a long strip of shimmery fabric or wide ribbon and glue the center of it to the top sides of the cording.

For each shepherd's staff, cut a 12" length of wire. Fold over ½" at one end of the wire for the bottom of the staff. Bend a large curve at the top end and use a needle-nose pliers to spiral the end. Wrap a wire arm around the staff.

Finish the Pieces
For the cradle, cut two 12" lengths of wire. With the spindles 1½" apart, center a wire over the spindles about ¾" from each end; wrap the wires around the spindles. Shape the wire into the legs of the cradle, spiraling the ends for the feet. Center the 10" length of 2½"-wide ribbon over the top of the cradle, bending the ribbon to follow the shape of the cradle. Place the Baby Jesus on the cradle.

Wrap two of the gifts with scraps of shimmery fabric. Glue the fabric in place or tie ribbon around the fabric to secure. Add ribbon and cording to the remaining gift. Glue a glass bead to the top of the finials.♥

Designed by Heidi Boyd

Ho-Ho-Homespun

When it comes to homemade for the holidays, a great place to start is in the sewing room! Rummage through fabric and felt scraps, carded buttons, spools of thread, and dressmaking trims. Look for such items as measuring tapes and flashy tassels, too. Use these goodies to create a theme as merry to look at as it is to make. Brightly adorned for the holidays, this evergreen sparkles with bold colors and treats, *opposite*. Tied to the highest branch, an eight-point topper shines with rainbow colors and buttons over the Christmas scene. Below, the tree is arrayed in crazy-quilt balls, cork reindeer, felt ornaments, God's-eye trims, and gingerbread kids. Tape-measure garlands inch their way around the tree. Instructions begin on *page 48.*

To craft the jolliest holiday ever, let bold-and-bright decor take center stage. For example, on this clever felt stocking, *left*, button-box finds play a starring role. In a colorful burst of buttons and appliqued felt, the stocking sets up a fanciful play of shapes and textures, placing pinked edges against rolling rickrack and polished pearl cotton.

Look what you can "grow" with copper wire! Potted in a papier-mâché box (or a vintage tin), this tiny tree gets firmly rooted in a poured plaster of Paris base, *opposite*. Its coiled branches open to button blooms, making it bright as a brand-new penny.

Rows of rickrack in assorted sizes and colors run circles around the rim of this playful tree skirt, *above*. Loaded with felt rounds and big buttons, it's got enough pizzazz to hold its own against the brightly ornamented tree, *opposite*. Use pinking shears to cut out the felt shapes and mimic the rickrack edge.

Let the kids get in on the act—they'll delight in helping craft these homespun tree treasures—all made from sewing box staples. At *left* in the photo *opposite*, feather stitches put a spin on a tasseled "beachball" bauble; in the *center,* pearl cotton wraps up a whimsical cork-and-dowel reindeer; at *right,* ribbon, cording, and floss turn a beaded snowflake into a merry God's-eye trimming.

Ho-Ho-Homespun

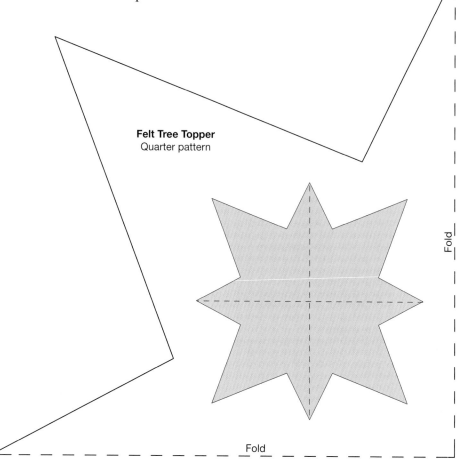

Felt Tree Topper
Quarter pattern

Fold

Fold

Felt Tree Topper
Shown on pages 42–43.

YOU WILL NEED
Graph paper
Felt: 12" square each of yellow, orange, red, and blue, and one 2¼"-diameter circle of purple
Pinking shears
Sewing threads, including purple and yellow
10 assorted buttons, ½"–1½"- diameter
Polyester fiberfill
1 yard of 1½"-wide red felt ribbon

INSTRUCTIONS
Trace and complete the star pattern, *above*, on folded tracing paper. Cut out the pattern piece. Use the star pattern and the pinking shears to cut one star from the yellow felt. Pin the yellow star on the orange felt; cut out one orange star about ⅛" beyond the edges of the yellow star. Use the orange star as a pattern to cut one slightly larger red star and the red star as a pattern to cut one slightly larger blue star. Cut a 3" slit in the center of the blue star for stuffing.

Center the purple felt circle on the yellow star. Use purple sewing thread to sew the circle in place about ⅛" from its outer edge. Referring to the photo on *page 42,* sew the buttons to the yellow star with contrasting threads.

Layer the stars from largest to smallest with the yellow star, right side up, on top. Use yellow sewing thread to sew the stars together about ⅛" from the outside edges of the yellow star. Stuff the tree topper with polyester stuffing through the 3" slit in the blue star. Whipstitch the opening closed.

Cut the felt ribbon in half. Center the ribbon lengths over the back of the star with one at the center and one at the top point. Hand-sew in place; trim the ribbon ends, and tie to secure star at top of tree.♥

Designed by Nancy Wyatt

Button Christmas Tree
Shown opposite and on page 44.

YOU WILL NEED
3×5½" round papier-mâché box
Goop adhesive
All-purpose spray enamel primer
Red satin latex spray paint
24" length of ⅝"-wide green grosgrain ribbon
115 assorted buttons, ⅜"–⅝"-diameter
38 yards of 24-gauge copper wire
Wire cutters
Needle-nose pliers
13" length of ⅛"-diameter brazing rod
Pencils
Plaster of Paris
Empty 8-ounce plastic tub to fit inside box
Masking tape
Green tissue paper
1 yard of ⅜"-wide ribbon

INSTRUCTIONS
Glue the lid to the box bottom and let the glue dry. Spray all surfaces of the box with enamel primer. When the primer is dry, spray all surfaces of the box with red satin paint. Let the paint dry.

Center and glue the green grosgrain ribbon on the sides of the lid, cutting the ribbon ends to overlap ½". Glue assorted buttons to the ribbon, leaving about ¼" space between the buttons.

From the copper wire, cut:
- 2—9" lengths
- 2—12" lengths
- 3—17" lengths
- 5—21" lengths
- 3—25" lengths
- 2—29" lengths
- 2—33" lengths
- 26—37" lengths

To make a double-branch, thread a button onto a wire and fold the wire in half with the button at the fold. Twist the wire together below the button, stopping 1" from the opposite end. Thread a second button onto one wire end; then twist the wire ends

together to secure. Use the needle-nose pliers to bend the twisted wire ends into one of the button holes. Repeat with each wire.

For the treetop, select the five shortest double branches. Place the button ends of the wires at one end of the brazing rod. Twist the wires around the rod to secure. Bend the wires and fan out the buttons to fill in the treetop.

Wrap the next shortest double branch around a pencil, forming a coil. Remove the pencil. Beginning just below the attached branches, wrap the center of this double branch around the rod. Repeat to attach all the double branches, working from the shortest to the longest as you go down the rod. The branches should cover about the top 10" of the rod.

Mix Plaster of Paris, following the instructions on the package. Pour the mixture into the plastic tub. Insert the bottom of the tree into the center of the tub. If necessary, prop up the tree with pencils crossed and taped to the sides of the tub. Let the plaster set up until dry; remove the pencils.

Place the tub into the box. Wrap tissue paper around the base of the tree for the tree skirt. Bend the branches as desired to shape the tree. Tie a bow at the center of the 1-yard length of ribbon. Place the bow at the top of the tree and drape the ribbon ends in the branches.♥

Designed by Kristin Detrick

Felt Tree Skirt
Shown on pages 43 and 46.

YOU WILL NEED
1¼ yards of 72"-wide red felt
9×12" pieces of felt in a variety of colors
T-pin; chalk pencil
1 yard of string
Pinking shears
Yardstick
3¾ yards each of small, medium, and jumbo rickrack trims
Matching sewing threads
30 assorted buttons, ranging from ⅞"- to 1½"-diameter
Assorted pearl cottons
3 yards of 1"-wide red grosgrain ribbon

INSTRUCTIONS
Fold the red felt in half. Find the center of the folded edge and mark it with a chalk pencil. Tie one end of string to the T-pin. Tie the remaining end of string to the chalk pencil, keeping 22" of string between the T-pin and pencil. Anchor the T-pin to the mark on the folded edge. Draw a semicircle on the felt with the chalk pencil by making an arc with the string fully extended.

For the tree-trunk opening, shorten the length of string between the pen and T-pin to 2½"; make a semicircle. Cut through both layers of felt on the marked lines, using pinking shears on the outer line. Unfold the felt. Mark the center back opening, using a yardstick to draw a line from the center to the outer edge. Cut on the center back line.

Pin the jumbo rickrack to the tree skirt about ½" from the outer edge; sew in place with matching sewing thread. Sew the medium and small rickrack to the skirt with matching sewing threads, leaving about ¾" between the trims.

From the assorted felts, use pinking shears to cut approximately 12—2"-diameter circles and 10—4"-diameter circles. Arrange the felt circles on the tree skirt inside the rickrack border. Use red sewing thread to sew the circles in place about ¼" from their outer edges. Arrange the buttons on the tree skirt; sew them in place with pearl cotton.

Cut the ribbon into six 18" lengths. Pin the ribbons in pairs along the left and right center back edges, positioning them at the top, bottom, and in the center. Sew in place; trim the ribbon ends, and tie into bows to secure the skirt around the tree.♥

Designed by Nancy Wyatt

Felt Stocking
Shown on pages 43 and 45.

YOU WILL NEED
Graph paper
Felt: ⅝ yard of red or green, ¼ yard of green or red, and assorted scraps
Pinking shears
Red, green, and white sewing threads
9 assorted buttons, ¾"-⅞"-diameter
Various sizes and colors of pearl cottons
Scrap paper
Tissue wrapping paper
Embroidery needle
½ yard of white jumbo rickrack

INSTRUCTIONS
Enlarge the stocking pattern, *page 50,* onto graph paper. Cut out the pattern.

Cut the Felt
From the red or green felt, cut two stockings. From the green or red felt, cut one 4½×15½" strip for the cuff and one ½×6" strip for the hanging loop. From the assorted felt scraps, use pinking shears to cut eight 2"-diameter circles.

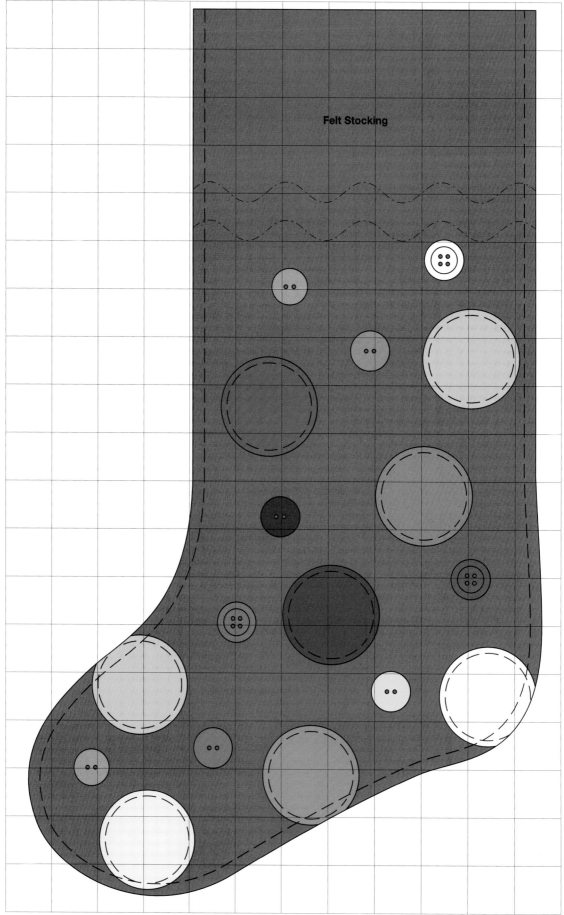

Felt Stocking

1 Square = 1 Inch

Ho-Ho-Homespun

Sew the Stocking

Arrange the felt circles on the stocking front. Use red or green sewing thread to sew the circles in place about ⅛" from their outer edges. Arrange the buttons on the stocking; sew and tie them in place with pearl cottons.

With wrong sides together, center the stocking front on the stocking back; pin together. Use red or green thread to top-stitch ¼" from the side and foot edges, leaving the top edge open. Pink the sewn edges.

Pink the long edges of the ½×6" hanging loop strip. Fold the strip in half, forming the loop. Sew the ends to the top outside corner on the heel side of the stocking with the loop above the stocking.

To personalize the stocking, practice writing the desired name on scrap paper to fit across the front of the cuff. When you are pleased with the name, trace it onto the tissue wrapping paper. Center the tissue pattern on the 4½×15½" cuff strip; pin in place. Use one strand of yellow-gold pearl cotton to stem-stitch through the tissue pattern and felt. When the embroidery is finished, carefully tear away the tissue wrapping paper.

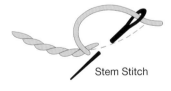

Stem Stitch

Sew the white jumbo rickrack along the bottom edge of the cuff. Use the pinking shears to finish the top edge of the cuff. With right sides facing, sew together the short edges of the cuff with a ¼" seam allowance. Turn the cuff right side out. Slip the cuff over the stocking with the wrong side of the cuff facing the right side of the stocking. Use red or green thread to top-stitch the cuff to the stocking ¼" from the top edges.♥

Designed by Nancy Wyatt

Beaded God's-Eye Ornament

Shown at right and on page 47.

YOU WILL NEED

22- and 24-gauge colored wires
Wire cutters
Embroidery floss
Narrow cord
¼"-wide satin ribbon
4–6 types of assorted color and shape wooden beads and/or miniature spools: 6 of each color and bead type
Glue gun and hotmelt adhesive
Needle-nose pliers

INSTRUCTIONS

Use the wire cutters to cut three 8" lengths of 22-gauge wire and one 2½" length of 24-gauge wire. Wrap the 2½" wire around the center of the 8" wires, evenly separating the long wires like spokes as you wrap.

Cut a 24" length of embroidery floss. Knot one end of the floss around the base of one of the wire spokes. Working in a clockwise direction, wrap the floss over and around each spoke; tie the end to the nearest spoke. Thread a bead on each of the six spokes.

To attach the cord, pull one end of the cord through the last matching bead before threading it on the final spoke. Apply a dot of glue to secure the cord end to the bead. Wrap the cord three times over and around the spokes, working in a clockwise direction. Pull the cord end through a new style of bead and thread the bead on the spoke; glue and trim the cord. Thread a matching bead on each remaining spoke.

Fold and glue one end of the ¼"-wide satin ribbon around a spoke. Wrap the ribbon two times over and around the spokes, working in a clockwise direction. Cut the ribbon; fold and glue the end around the spoke. Thread a new bead style onto each spoke. Add beads until 1" of wire spoke remains. Use needle-nose pliers to bend each wire end, forming a loop and securing the beads.

For the hanging loop, cut a 9" length of cord or ¼"-wide satin ribbon. Thread the cord or ribbon through one of the wire loops; knot the ends of the ribbon together.♥

Designed by Heidi Boyd

Felt Ball Ornament

Shown on page 47.

YOU WILL NEED

Tracing paper
4"-diameter Styrofoam ball
6 assorted felt scraps
Assorted pearl cottons
Straight pins
Embroidery needle
Purchased 2½"-long tassel

INSTRUCTIONS

Trace the pattern, *page 52,* onto tracing paper; cut out the pattern piece. Use the pattern to cut one shape from six assorted felt scraps.

For the hanging loop, cut two 30" lengths of pearl cotton. Combine the cut lengths into a single strand. Secure one end of the joined strands and twist until tightly wound. Holding the ends, fold the strand in half as the two halves twist around each other. Knot both ends to secure them. Fold the twisted pearl cotton in half and tie a knot about 4" from the fold, forming the loop. Trim off the excess about 1" below the knot.

Arrange the felt pieces on the ball, using the straight pins to hold them

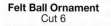

Felt Ball Ornament
Cut 6

Reindeer Ornament
Shown below.

YOU WILL NEED
Standard cork, such as from a wine bottle
Small and medium bottle corks
5 assorted buttons
Size 3 pearl cotton
Glue gun and hotmelt adhesive
20-gauge colored wire
Wire cutters
Needle-nose pliers
Bamboo skewer
20" length of cording

INSTRUCTIONS
For the body, hot-glue buttons to both ends of the standard cork. Hot-glue an end of the pearl cotton to the button rim at one end of the body. Tightly wrap the pearl cotton around the body, applying glue to the cork as you work. Continue to the button rim at the opposite end, covering the cork completely. Do not cut the pearl cotton yet.

Hot-glue the wider end of the small cork to the body for the neck. Bring the pearl cotton to the base of the neck; wrap and glue the pearl cotton around the neck to cover it. Cut the pearl cotton and carefully hot-glue the end to the top of the neck.

For the head, hot-glue buttons to the ends of the medium cork and wrap as for the body. Glue the head to the top of the neck. Use the wire cutters to cut two 4" lengths of colored wire. Bend each wire length into an antler with the needle-nose pliers. Pierce the top of the head with the ends of the antlers; glue in place. Hot-glue a small button to the end of the head for the nose.

From the bamboo skewer, cut four 2"-long pieces for the legs. Hot-glue pearl cotton around each leg and glue the legs to the underside of the body. For the tail, cut a 2½" length of wire. Use the needle-nose pliers to shape the wire into a tight curl. Glue one end of the tail into a buttonhole at the back of the body.

For the hanging loop, fold the 20" length of cording in half. Tie a knot in the cording about 4" from the fold, forming the loop. With the knot against the back of the neck, tie the cording into a bow around the neck front.♥
Designed by Heidi Boyd

Measuring Tape Garland
Shown at left and on page 47.

YOU WILL NEED
3½ yards of 1½"-wide wire-edge plaid ribbon
120" measuring tape
Glue gun and hotmelt adhesive
5 plastic darning needles
Silver paint marker
5 wooden spools
5—30" lengths of ¼"-wide satin ribbon in assorted colors
Variety of buttons

INSTRUCTIONS
Hot-glue the measuring tape centered on the ribbon for the garland. Trim the ribbon ends at an angle. Use the silver paint marker to color the plastic needles; let the paint dry. For the

in place. Pin the hanging loop at the center top of the ornament and the tassel at the center button; tuck the ends underneath the felt pieces. Use a variety of pearl cottons and herringbone stitches to sew the felt pieces together, securing the hanging loop and tassel in your stitches.♥
Designed by Nancy Wyatt

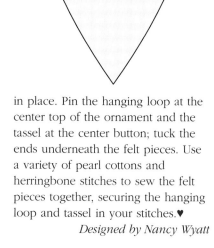

Herringbone Stitch

Ho-Ho-Homespun

thread, hot-glue one end of each ¼"-wide ribbon to the center of a wooden spool. Wind the ribbon around the spool. Thread each remaining ribbon end through a needle. Stretch the garland out on a flat surface and arrange the spools and needles on the front as desired. Hot-glue the spools and needles in place, letting the ribbon curl and drape over the garland. Tack the ribbon with glue. Randomly hot-glue buttons to the garland.♥

Designed by Heidi Boyd

Gingerbread Boy and Girl Ornaments
Shown at right and on page 43.

YOU WILL NEED

For boy and girl:
Tracing paper
Felt: 1 sheet each of adhesive tan and stiff white and a scrap of red
2—12" lengths of 20-gauge brass wire
Assorted buttons
Craft yarn in assorted colors
Glue gun and hotmelt adhesive
Pom-poms for the eyes, the noses, the buttons, and the shoes
Pearl cotton: red and gold
Rickrack trims
Crafts glue

INSTRUCTIONS

Trace the boy and girl of your choice, and bow patterns, *page 54,* onto tracing paper. Cut out the pattern pieces. Cut each body pattern from both tan and white felt. Cut the bow from red or white felt.

For the hanging loop, thread 4 to 5 buttons on a 12" length of wire. Position the buttons along the wire by rotating each button three times to twist the wire around each button. Shape the wire, placing the wire ends over the hands on the front of the white body. Remove the paper backing from the tan body. Center the tan body, adhesive side down, on the white body, trapping the wire end between the felt layers.

Hot-glue craft yarn around the edges of each body. Glue craft yarn hair and the felt bow on the girl. Cut a small piece of pearl cotton for the mouth. Glue the mouth, small pom-pom nose, and pom-pom eyes on the faces. Refer to the photographs *above* and on *page 43,* as guides for the clothing, adding buttons, rickrack, and yarn.♥

Designed by Heidi Boyd

Felt Ornaments
Shown on pages 43 and 55.

YOU WILL NEED

Tracing paper
Kunin Rainbow Felt: 9×12" pieces of Antique White, Apple Green, Cadet Blue, Gold, and Red
Assorted buttons, ranging from ¼" to ⅝"-diameter
Cotton embroidery floss: blue, green, red, white, and yellow
Embroidery needles
⅛"-wide ribbon or clothespins and crafts glue

INSTRUCTIONS

Trace the patterns on *pages 56* and *57* onto tracing paper. Cut out each pattern piece.

Cut the Felt

For the ornaments, use the pattern pieces to cut the shapes from a variety of felt colors, referring to the photos on *page 43* and on *page 55* for color suggestions. Use a different color of felt for the front and back of each ornament. Cut an appliqué motif for each ornament front, using one heart, or one large star, or one tree and one small star.

For one mitten ornament, cut two mittens, two mitten cuffs, and one appliqué motif.

For one stocking ornament, cut two stockings, two stocking cuffs, two stocking tops, one toe, and one appliqué motif.

For one hat ornament, cut two hats, two hat brims, two tassels, and one appliqué motif.

Sew the Ornaments

Use six plies of floss for all of the embroidery stitches and to sew on the buttons. Select a contrasting floss color so the stitches are easily visible.

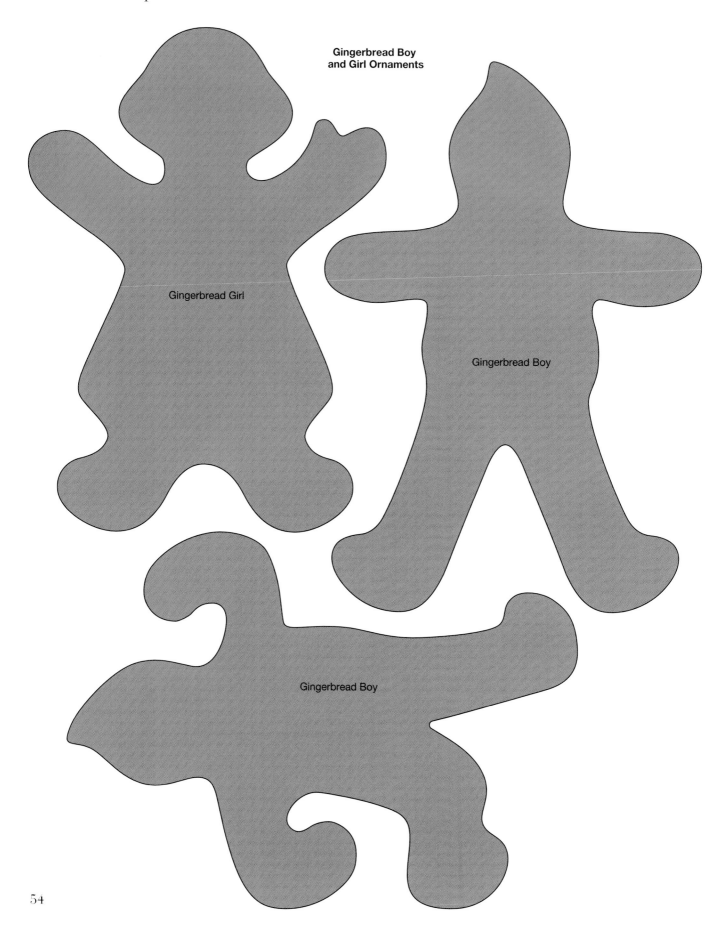

**Gingerbread Boy
and Girl Ornaments**

Gingerbread Girl

Gingerbread Boy

Gingerbread Boy

Position and pin the desired appliqué motif on the ornament front. Sew the motif to the ornament front, blanket-stitching along all edges of the heart and straight-stitching along all edges of the large star or tree and small star. Sew small buttons to each point of the large star and to decorate the tree. Add a button to the center bottom of the tree for the tree trunk.

Hat Ornament. With right sides facing, hand- or machine-sew the hat front to the hat back using a scant ⅛" seam allowance and leaving the bottom edge open. Turn the hat right side out.

Position and pin a hat brim on the right side of the hat front with the bottom edges even. To attach the brim, sew a row of four buttons along the bottom edge, sewing through both layers of felt. Repeat for the hat back to attach the remaining hat brim.

To make a tassel, roll the tassel piece widthwise. Knot a 4" length of floss around the center of the rolled tassel; do not trim the floss ends. Fold the tassel in half, bringing the cut felt ends together at the bottom and the floss ends at the top. Wrap a second length of floss around the tassel about ½" below the fold; knot and

trim the ends. Make a second tassel. Use the floss ends to sew a tassel to each point of the hat.

Mitten Ornament. Position and pin a mitten cuff on the wrong side of the mitten front with the mitten overlapping the cuff. To attach the cuff, sew a row of three to five buttons along the bottom edge of the mitten front, sewing through both layers of felt. Repeat for the mitten back and the remaining mitten cuff, using two buttons.

With right sides facing, hand- or machine-sew the mitten front to the mitten back using a scant ⅛" seam allowance and leaving the cuff edge open. Turn the mitten right side out.

Stocking Ornament. Position and pin a toe to the stocking front. Straight-stitch along the straight edge of the toe piece. Position and pin a stocking cuff to the wrong side of the stocking front with the stocking overlapping

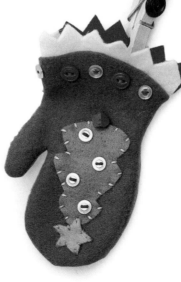

the cuff. Straight-stitch along the zigzag edge of the stocking. Position and pin the stocking top to the wrong side of the stocking cuff with the cuff overlapping the top. To attach the top, sew a row of four to five buttons along the top edge of the stocking cuff, sewing through both layers of felt. Repeat for the stocking back and the remaining stocking cuff and stocking top.

With right sides facing, hand- or machine-sew the stocking front to the stocking back using a scant ⅛" seam allowance and leaving the cuff edge open. Turn the stocking right side out.

Finish the Ornaments

For a hanging loop, cut a 12" length of ⅛"-wide ribbon. Thread the ribbon ends through a large-eye embroidery needle. Insert the needle at the center top of the ornament and pull the ribbon ends only to the inside of the ornament. Knot the ribbon ends together on the inside.

To make a clothespin hanger, glue several buttons to the front of a clothespin. Let the glue dry. Use the clothespin to hang the ornaments on the tree branches.♥

Designed by Heidi Boyd

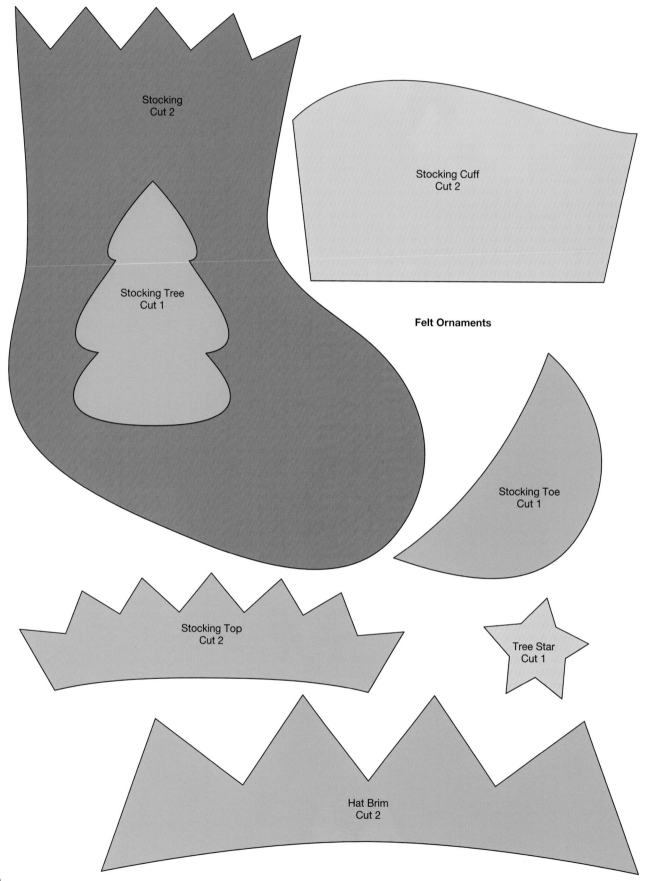

Stocking
Cut 2

Stocking Cuff
Cut 2

Felt Ornaments

Stocking Tree
Cut 1

Stocking Toe
Cut 1

Stocking Top
Cut 2

Tree Star
Cut 1

Hat Brim
Cut 2

Felt Ornaments

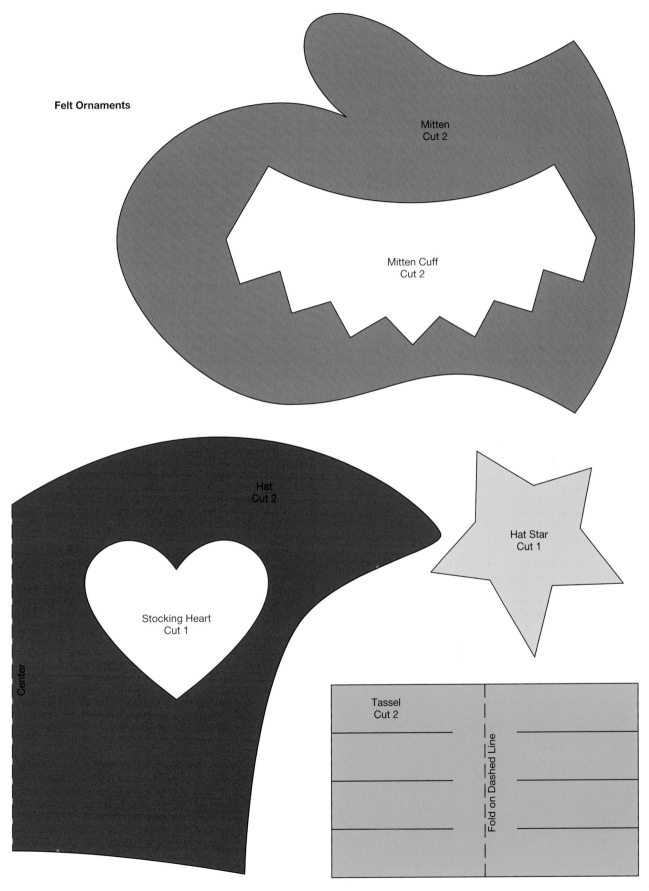

Mitten
Cut 2

Mitten Cuff
Cut 2

Hat
Cut 2

Hat Star
Cut 1

Stocking Heart
Cut 1

Center

Tassel
Cut 2

Fold on Dashed Line

Santa's Workshop

Kids just can't wait for the holidays. So let the festivities begin with a surprise: a Santa's workshop of their very own. This diminutive tree, *opposite,* is packed full of ornaments excited children will enjoy making while anticipating Santa's arrival. Let little elves thread wood shapes and beads onto boot laces for Santa and reindeer figurines. Help them make Santa's list and letters next; use shrinking art paper to bring them down to ornament size. Then kick the fun into high gear with a candy garland that looks nearly yummy enough to eat and Santa boots (look who's inside), all made from modeling compound. For more ornaments, turn the page. Instructions begin on *page 62.*

Look who's at work—and play—around the base of this child-size Christmas tree, *opposite*. Crafted from felt, chenille stems, and beads, Santa's helper elves put the finishing touches on a collection of tiny wood toys.

The toys are preassembled, so all your little ones need to do is partially paint them. See the pom-pom-and-toothpick paintbrush in each elf's hand? Be sure to dip the tips into paint so the elves keep busy.

Kids will delight in hanging Santa's "laundry" on the tree, *opposite, above,* and *below*. Cut from red and white felt, the classic fur-trimmed coat, mittens, hat, and even Santa's longjohns get hung up to dry on clever paper-clip hangers.

Santa's Workshop

All designs were created by Heidi Boyd.

Santa's Boots Ornaments
Shown below and on pages 58 and 59.

YOU WILL NEED

Waxed paper
Sculpey III polymer clay: black, chocolate, copper, tan, and white
Crafts knife
Pencil
Table knife
Seed beads: 2 small for the eyes and 1 large for the nose
Needle or toothpick
Bobby pin
Baking sheet
Aluminum foil
12" length of 1"-wide ribbon

INSTRUCTIONS

Cover your work area with a sheet of waxed paper. Knead the clay between the palms of your hands until it is soft and pliable.

For the boots, roll the black clay into a 1"-diameter log; then cut a 3"-long piece for each boot. Bend 1" of clay up at a 90-degree angle to create the foot of the boot, rounding the toe end. For the heels, roll two pea-sized balls of black; flatten the balls. Press the heels onto the bottom of the boot.

Use a pencil to make the opening in the top of each boot.

For the fur, roll a ½"-diameter log of white clay. Flatten the log and wrap it around the top edge of each boot. To give the fur texture, push the table knife tip into the clay and use a short, quick motion to spread the white clay over the top edge of the black clay. Continue to add texture to all the white clay.

Place the boots side by side and firmly press them together, blending the edges.

For the cat, roll a dime-sized ball of copper clay; pinch two ears at the top of the head. For the dog, roll a small egg shape of chocolate clay; form two floppy ears at the top of the head. To add stripes or spots, roll tiny balls or coils of a contrasting color, using Tan for the dog and white for the cat. Flatten them on your work surface and gently press the flattened spot or stripe on the animal.

For the front animal legs, roll a ¼"-diameter log of clay; cut two ¾"-long pieces. Gently blend one end of the legs onto the base of the head. Use the needle or toothpick to position the beads on the face. Use two small seed beads for the eyes and one larger seed bead for the nose; insert the nose bead on its side. Use the side of the needle or toothpick to define the paws. Place the pet into the top of the boot, blending the clay slightly to anchor. For the tail, roll a thin snake. Cut it to the desired length and press it into the back of the animal.

Insert the open end of a bobby pin into the center back of the boots until only ¼" remains at the top. Place the ornament on a baking sheet covered with aluminum foil. Put the baking sheet in the oven and bake the ornament according to the instructions on the clay package.

When the ornament is cool to the touch, thread the ribbon through the bobby pin; knot the ends together.♥

Santa's List & Envelope Ornaments
Shown right and on page 59.

YOU WILL NEED

White paper
8×10" sheets of Shrinky Dinks Frosted Ruff n' Ready shrinkable plastic
Sharpie permanent markers
Colored pencils
Paper punch
6" length of cord or narrow ribbon
Small feathers (about 2" long)
Glue gun and hotmelt adhesive

INSTRUCTIONS

Trace Santa's List pattern, *opposite,* onto a sheet of white paper, and personalize with family names and wishes. For the envelope, draw a 5×8" rectangle on a sheet of white paper. Decorate the rectangle, referring to the photograph on *page 59* as a guide. When making your pattern, consider that it will shrink to about one-third of its original size.

Place a sheet of shrinkable plastic, shiny side facing up, over the pattern on a flat surface. Use permanent markers to trace and color the design onto the front of the plastic, drawing directly over your pattern lines. Cut out the list and envelope shapes. Use colored pencils on the back of the design to darkly shade the edges.

Punch a hole near an edge of the design for hanging. Bake the ornament, following the package instructions. When the ornament is cool, thread cord or ribbon through the hole and knot the ends together. For Santa's pen, hot-glue a small feather to the bottom of the list.♥

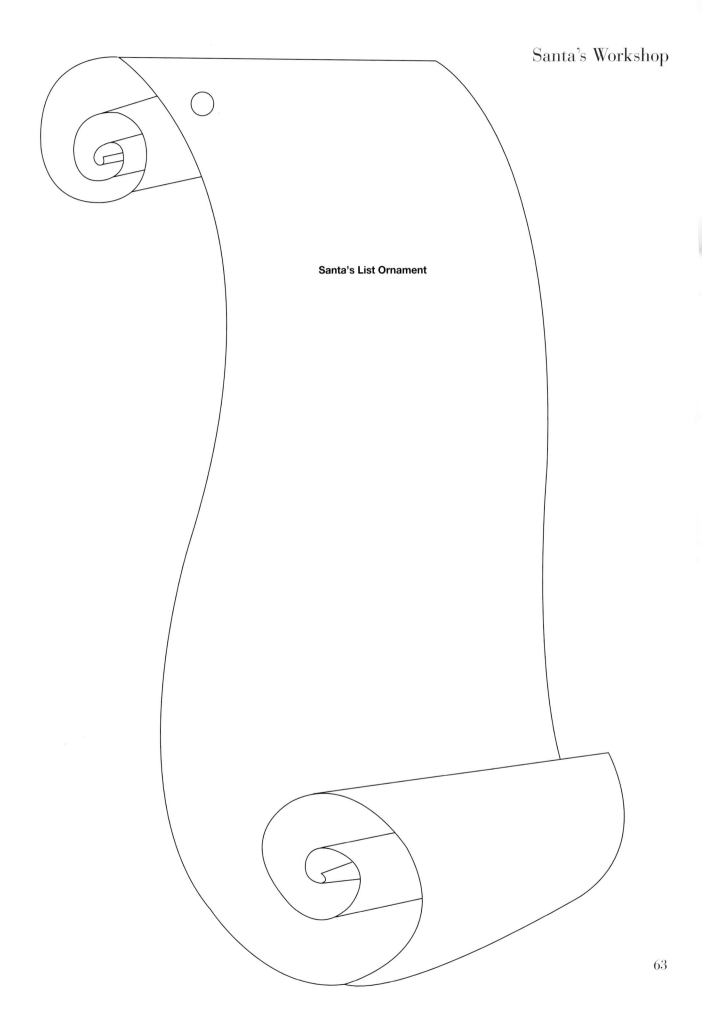

Santa's List Ornament

Santa's Workshop

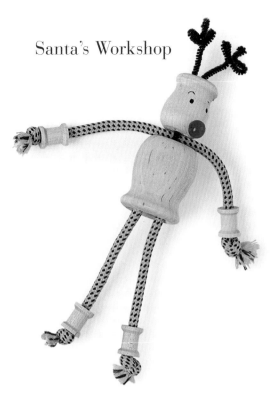

Reindeer Ornament
Shown above and on page 59.

YOU WILL NEED
Wooden candle cups: 1 large for the body and 1 small for the head
4 small wooden spools for the hooves
1 small red bead for the nose
Yellow-and-brown bootlaces
Brown chenille stem
Black permanent marker
Glue gun and hotmelt adhesive

INSTRUCTIONS
Cut a 10½" length of bootlace for the legs and a 7½" length for the arms, including a hard plastic end on each length. Thread two spools on each length of bootlace. Trim the plastic end; tie a knot at each end of the laces. Position a spool against each knot.

To assemble the reindeer, fold the brown chenille stem in half. Position the center of the legs at the fold of the chenille stem. Thread the stem ends through the inverted large candle cup. Slip the center of the arms between the stem ends at the top of the large candle cup. Thread the stem ends through the bottom of the small candle cup. Separate the stem ends and shape each into an antler.

Use the black marker to draw the eyes and eyebrows on the face. For the nose, hot-glue a red bead to the center bottom of the face.♥

Santa Ornament
Shown below and on page 59.

YOU WILL NEED
Wooden thimble for the hat
Wooden round beads: 1 large for the head and 2 small for the hands
Wooden candle cups: 1 large for the body and 2 small for the upper legs
2 wooden plant pots for the boots
2 small wooden wheels for the boots
Acrylic paint: red, black, and white
Paintbrush
Red-and-black bootlaces
Black chenille stem
Glue gun and hotmelt adhesive
Small white pom-pom
White looped chenille stem

INSTRUCTIONS
Paint the wheels and the plant pots black. Paint the candle cups and the thimble red. Let the paint dry.

For the legs, cut a 16" length of bootlace, including a hard plastic end in the measurement. Tie a knot at the cut end of the lace. For the first boot, thread a wheel and a plant pot on the plastic end of the lace with the pot bottom toward the wheel. Slide the pieces down the lace until the wheel is against the knot. Make a knot in the lace 2" above the boot. For the upper legs, thread an inverted small candle cup on the lace to sit on the knot. Then thread a second small candle cup, right side up, on the lace. Make a knot in the lace 2" from the last knot for the second candle cup. For the second boot, thread on a plant pot and a wheel. Knot the lace below the boot, leaving 2" between the last knot and the top of the boot. Trim off the plastic end of the lace.

For the arms, cut an 8" length of bootlace, including a plastic end in the measurement. For the hands, thread on two small beads. Trim off the plastic end; tie a knot at each end of the lace. Position a bead against each knot.

To assemble Santa, fold the black chenille stem in half. Position the center of the legs at the fold of the chenille stem. Thread the stem ends through the bottom of the large candle cup. Twist the stem around the center of the arms. Hot-glue the stem ends inside the round head bead. Invert; then hot-glue the thimble on top of Santa's head. Glue the white pom-pom to the top of the hat.

For the beard, fold a 2" length of white looped chenille stem in half. Glue the beard to the bottom of the head bead and the top of the candle cup body. Paint the eyes and eyebrows black. Mix a little red with white paint. Use this mixture for the cheeks and nose.♥

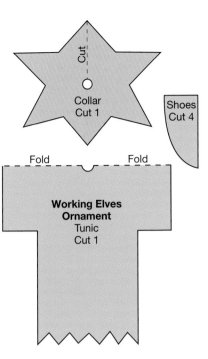

Working Elves Ornaments

Shown on pages 59 and 60.

YOU WILL NEED

For each ornament:

Tracing paper

Green and red felt

Chenille stems: 2 beige for body and
    1 red or green for hat

Red and green pearl cotton

Small wooden round bead for the head

Crafts glue

Pre-assembled wooden toy

Red and green acrylic paint

Black permanent marker

Toothpicks

Pom-poms: 1 small red or green, and
    1 tiny white

Glue gun and hotmelt adhesive

INSTRUCTIONS

Trace the patterns, *above,* onto tracing paper. Cut out each pattern piece. Use the pattern pieces to cut one tunic, four shoes, and one collar from the felt, using a different color of felt for the collar and tunic.

For the elf's body, fold one beige chenille stem in half; the fold is for the head. Fold up 2" at each stem end, creating a doubled-stem for the legs. For the arms, cut a 9" length from the second beige stem and wrap the center around the first stem about ½" below the top fold. Fold in 2" at each end toward the body, doubling the stem. Tightly wrap pearl cotton around the arms and legs, completely covering the stems except for the hands. Glue the ends of the pearl cotton to secure. To make stripes on the legs, wrap a second color of pearl cotton over the first color.

For the feet, bend about ¼" forward at the bottom of each leg. Glue the felt shoe pieces together in pairs, sandwiching a foot between each pair. Cut the hole at the center of the tunic as indicated on the pattern. Slip the tunic over the body, inserting the top fold of the stem through the hole. Glue the slides and underarm area of

the tunic together to cover the stem. Glue the round bead on the top fold of the stem. Place the collar over the tunic, and glue at the center front and back. For the hat, apply glue to the top of the head. Wrap the chenille stem around the glued area of the head and then continue to wrap the stem upward. Glue a small pom-pom to the tip of the hat. Use the black marker to draw eyes on the face.

For the paintbrush, slightly shorten a toothpick and glue a tiny white pompom to the end. Partially paint the wooden toy and dip the bottom of the white pom-pom in the same paint color. Let the paint dry.

Position the elf on the wooden toy, bending the knees and elbows as desired. Push the end of the paintbrush through the fold at one hand. Hot-glue the elf and the tip of the paintbrush in place.♥

Santa's Laundry Ornaments

Shown on pages 59 and 61.

YOU WILL NEED

Tracing paper

Stiffened red and white felt

Black and white beads

Large silver paper clips

Miniature wood clothespins

Tacky glue

Needle-nose pliers

INSTRUCTIONS

Trace the patterns, *below* and on *page 66,* onto tracing paper. Cut out the pieces. Use the patterns to cut the long underwear, coat, mittens, and hat from stiffened red felt and all the fur shapes from stiffened white felt.

Use crafts glue to glue the fur shapes to the corresponding garments. For the buttons, glue four black beads to the center front of the coat and seven white beads to the center front of the long underwear.

For the hangers, reshape the large paper clips. Open the paper clip into a triangular shape, leaving the two outer manufactured bends in place as the base of the hanger. Use needle-nose pliers to shape the center bend at one end of the paper clip into the hanger hook, clamping the end with the pliers and pulling it into a curve. Bend back the opposite end. Pin the clothing on the hangers with miniature clothespins.♥

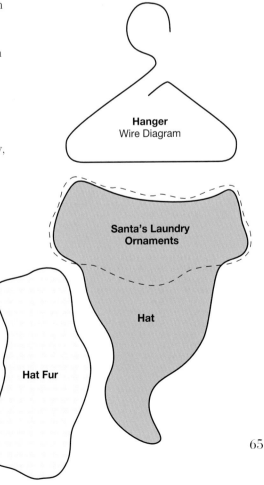

65

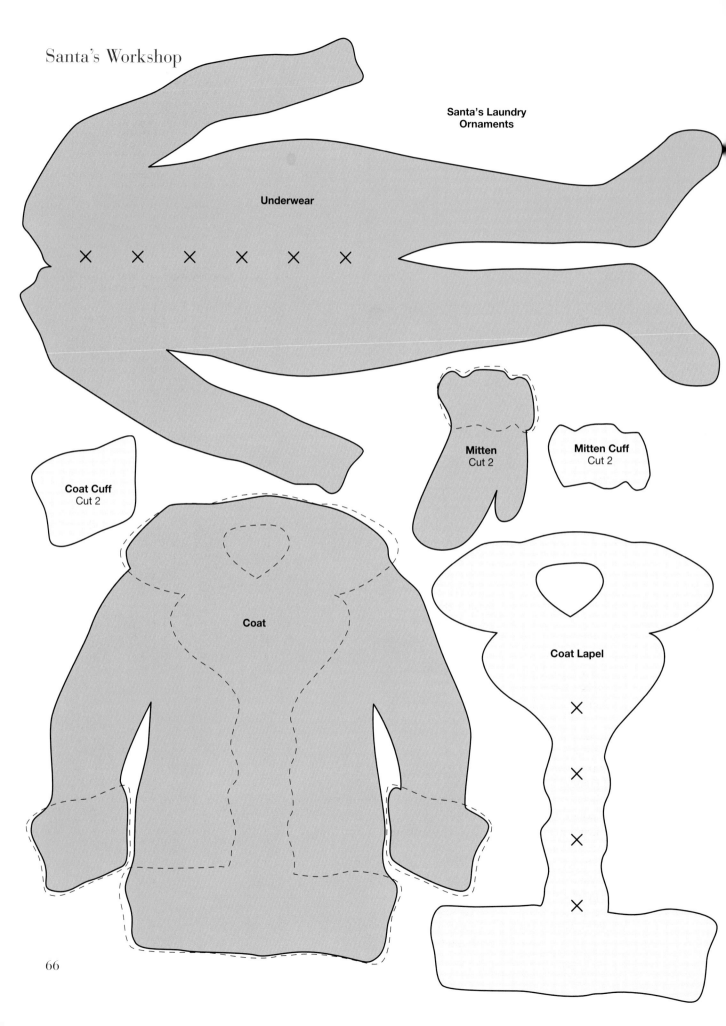

Santa's Laundry
Ornaments

Underwear

Mitten
Cut 2

Mitten Cuff
Cut 2

Coat Cuff
Cut 2

Coat

Coat Lapel

Candy Garland
Shown at right.

YOU WILL NEED

Waxed paper
Sculpey III polymer clay: green, red,
   white, and yellow
Miniature glass marbles: green, red,
   and clear
Small bowl
Darning needle or toothpick
Crafts knife
Butter knife
Straight-sided drinking glass
White plastic lacing
Baking sheet
Aluminum foil

INSTRUCTIONS

Cover your work area with a sheet of waxed paper. Knead the clay between the palms of your hands until it is soft and pliable.

For the gumdrops, roll a 1"-diameter ball of clay; flatten one side of the ball for the base. Pinch up the top of the ball to elongate the gumdrop tip. Gently roll the gumdrop on its side until the surface is smooth. Empty the desired color of miniature marbles into a small bowl. Press all surfaces of the gumdrop into the marbles. Apply pressure with your fingertips to firmly anchor the marbles in the clay. Use a darning needle or toothpick to make a hole through the center sides of the gumdrop.

For the peppermints, roll a 1"-diameter ball of white clay; gently flatten the ball into a 1½"-diameter circle for the candy base. Roll ¼"-diameter snakes of red and green clay. Flatten the snakes and cut 1½" lengths. To add the stripes, place the center of a flattened length over the edge of the base. The ends should almost reach the center of the base on the front and back. Press the stripe onto the base. Continue to add 5 or 6 more stripes around the base. Use the side of a butter knife and a circular motion to blend the stripe ends into the base. Use a darning needle or toothpick to make a hole through the candy from edge to edge.

For the ribbon candy, roll ½"-diameter, 12"-long logs of green, red, white, and yellow clay. Lay the logs side by side. Roll down the length of the logs with a straight-sided drinking glass, joining the logs together and increasing the length. Use a knife to cut a straight edge at the top and bottom. Cut the striped clay in half.

Accordion-fold each piece back and forth. Use a darning needle or toothpick to make a hole through the center of each ribbon candy.

For the hard candy squares, roll ½"-diameter logs of green, red, white, and yellow clay. Lay the logs side by side and firmly press them together, making a long block of clay. Cut the clay into square pieces. Use a darning needle or toothpick to make a hole through the candy from edge to edge.

Repeat the instructions to make as many candies as desired. Place the candies on a baking sheet covered with aluminum foil. Put the baking sheet in the oven and bake the candy according to the instructions on the clay package.

When the candies are cool to the touch, arrange them as desired, distributing the varieties and colors. Thread them onto the plastic lacing, making a knot before and after each candy to hold it in place on the garland. Our candies are spaced about 3½" apart.♥

Cedar Lodge

Collect some of nature's generous bounty for a Christmas grounded in woodsy aromas and rustic textures, *opposite*. Just before the snow flies, gather all the outdoorsy things you love best: pinecones, oak branches, mosses, acorns, pheasant feathers, and berries. Then bring this nature-rich collection into the midst of your holiday celebration.

Think this handsome stocking, *above*, is a time-consuming knitted project? The woolly design is much more easily made from an old winter pullover. Rather than toss a garment that's past its prime, cut out stocking pieces, maneuvering the prettiest sections for the cuff, toe, and heel. A quick stitch on the sewing machine "knits" the thrifty stocking into the fabric of your family's holiday traditions. Instructions begin on *page 74*.

Check out the ingenious canoe ornament, *above*. It isn't made of birch bark, and it won't float, but what a unique way to illuminate an outdoor theme! Emboss on the copper foil first; then cut out the shapes. Punch tiny holes along the bottom edges so you can lash the sides together. To raise the design and add earth-tone polish, use paint to accent the embossed areas.

Natural elements of copper, bronze, and silver infuse this fragrant pine, *opposite*, with glimmers of light. From sun-brushed accents on the acorn and pinecone garland, embossed fish-motif log slices, and map-covered photo frames to the brilliance of silver cross-country skis and copper canoes, the tree shimmers with natural bounty.

Let nature's abundant everlastings ring around a wreath of native beauty, *opposite*. Made in a calming, repetitive rhythm, the design has real down-to-earth attitude—the kind that's easily re-created or adapted from nature's infinite variety. When you're ready to lay the groundwork, select materials of rugged and varied textures. Here, sturdy twigs, white strawflowers, and tight-closed pinecones make a wonderful play against the more delicate edging of dried sweet Annie. Except for a row of red celosia and a bit of bright green moss, the composition is neutral. To keep the wreath eye-appealing, make sure it's rich in textural contrast.

Catch a fisherman's fancy with this miniature creel tree ornament, *above*. Filled with "keepers" made of painted and gilded foam fish shapes, the basket also sports a dowel rod-and-reel.

Sweater Stocking
Shown below and on page 69.

YOU WILL NEED
Graph paper
Tracing paper
Old sweater
Matching sewing thread
Assorted buttons or fine leather lacing
   and large-eye needle

INSTRUCTIONS
Enlarge the stocking pattern, *page 15,* onto graph paper. Cut out the pattern piece. To make heel and toe patterns, trace the toe and heel areas of the stocking pattern onto tracing paper; cut out the pattern pieces, adding ½" seam allowances at the inner edges. Sew all pieces with right sides together, using ½" seam allowances unless otherwise noted.

Cut the Fabric
Use the stocking pattern to cut two shapes from an old sweater for the stocking front and back, positioning the pattern to utilize the sweater's design and ribbing. Cut one heel and toe from the sweater if desired. To add a cuff, cut a 17" length of ribbing in the desired width from the sweater, using the finished bottom from the waist if desired. Cut a 2¼×7" strip for the hanging loop.

Sew the Stocking
With right sides together, sew the heel and toe to the stocking front. Fold the heel and toe pieces down over the stocking front, creating a double layer; baste together the outer edges.

Sew the stocking front to the back, leaving the top edge open. Press the seam allowances open as much as possible; turn right side out.

For the cuff, sew together the short edges of the 17" long strip, forming a circle. Press the seam allowances open. For a narrow cuff, press the cuff in half lengthwise with wrong sides together, matching the raw edges and seams. Slip the cuff onto the stocking, aligning the cuff seam with the heel seam and keeping the raw edges even; sew the cuff to the stocking with ¼" seam allowances. Turn up the cuff. Use the large-eye needle to weave leather lacing along the bottom edge of the narrow cuff; knot together the lacing ends. For a wide cuff, slip the cuff inside the stocking with the right side of the cuff facing the wrong side of the stocking. Sew the top edges of the stocking and cuff together, using ¼" seam allowances. Turn the cuff down over the stocking. Sew assorted buttons along the bottom front edge of the wide cuff.

For the hanging loop, fold in both long edges of the 2¼×7" strip to overlap at the center back of the strip. Hand-sew the edges in place. Fold the strip in half, forming the loop. Hand-sew the ends to the top inside corner on the heel side of the stocking. ♥

Designed by Mary Jo Hiney

Canoe Ornament
Shown on page 70.

YOU WILL NEED
Tracing paper
Copper tooling foil with wooden stylus
⅛" hole punch
Felt, or other soft surface, such as
   cardboard or newspaper
Tape
DecoArt No-Prep Metal paint: Coal Black
Paper towels
24" length of 20-gauge copper wire
9" length of leather lacing
Artificial holly leaves

INSTRUCTIONS
Trace the pattern *opposite* onto tracing paper; cut out the pattern piece. Unroll the copper metal sheet and place on felt. Lay the traced pattern over the metal and tape it in place. Use the pointed end of the wooden stylus to transfer the outline of the canoe onto the metal, drawing directly over the traced lines. Remove the pattern. Cut out the canoe with a scissors. Transfer and cut out a second canoe. Stack the two canoes, wrong sides facing, and use the hole punch to make holes through both layers ½" apart along the bottom edges of the canoe.

To add the embossed design along the top edge of the canoe, place each piece, right side down, on the felt. Position the pattern over the metal shape and use the pointed end of the stylus to transfer the design. Turn the piece over and outline the design with the stylus. Repeat with the second canoe piece.

To shape the canoe, place each piece, right side down, on the felt. Use the rounded end of the stylus to apply even pressure over the entire back of each canoe piece, avoiding the design areas.

Use paper towels to apply a small amount of metal paint onto the right side of each canoe piece. Wipe off the excess paint. Let the paint dry.

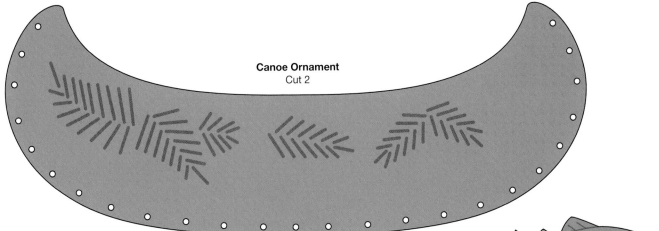

Canoe Ornament
Cut 2

Fish and Wood Ornament

With wrong sides together, align the canoe pieces, matching the holes. Use the wire to overhand-stitch the canoe pieces together. Trim the excess wire and bend the ends into the canoe.

For the hanging loop, thread one end of the leather lacing underneath the wire at one end of the canoe. Knot the lacing ends together. Wrap the artificial holly leaves around the base of the hanging loop.♥

Designed by Heidi Boyd

Fish and Wood Ornaments
Shown below.

YOU WILL NEED
2½–3"-diameter wood branch
Electric miter box saw or fine-toothed handsaw and miter box
Drill; ³⁄₁₆" and ¹⁄₁₆" drill bits
Leafing adhesive kit and silver metal leafing flakes
Tracing paper
Tape
36-gauge copper tooling foil
Ballpoint pen or embossing tool
Small, sharp manicure scissors
Goop adhesive
Acorns and small pinecones
Aluminum foil
Baking sheet
Size 4 screw eyes
Pliers
Aleene's All Purpose Primer
Small paintbrushes
Bronze acrylic paint
Small stencil sponge
Ultra-fine gold glitter
Jute twine
Red wooden beads
Glue gun and hotmelt adhesive

INSTRUCTIONS
Use the electric miter box saw or the handsaw to cut ¼"-wide slices from the wood branch. Use the drill and the ³⁄₁₆" drill bit to make a hole through the center top and center bottom of each wood slice about ⅜" from the edge. Apply adhesive and silver metal leafing flakes to the center of each wood slice, following the kit manufacturer's instructions.

Trace the fish pattern, *above right,* onto tracing paper. Lay the traced pattern over the copper foil and tape in place. Use a ballpoint pen or embossing tool to transfer the fish design onto the copper foil, drawing directly over the traced lines. Trace one fish for each wood slice. Cut out the copper fish with the manicure scissors. Use Goop adhesive to glue a fish centered over the silver leafing area on each wood slice.

Place the acorns and pinecones on an aluminum foil-lined baking sheet; bake in a 325° oven for 20 minutes. When the acorns and pinecones are cool, use the ¹⁄₁₆" drill bit to make a hole at the center top of each. Make a hole through the cap and just into the shell of each acorn and a ¼" deep hole in each pinecone. Insert a screw eye into each hole, using pliers if needed.

Use the paintbrush to coat the screw eyes with primer; let them dry. Paint each screw eye bronze with the stencil sponge. When the screw eyes are dry, sponge bronze paint onto an acorn or pinecone. Immediately sprinkle glitter lightly over the wet paint. Use a paintbrush to remove

any excess glitter. Continue to sponge paint and apply glitter to the acorns and pinecones one at a time.

For the hanging loop, cut a 13½" length of jute twine. Thread a length of twine through the top hole of each wood slice. Bring the twine ends together and thread the ends through one red bead. Slip the bead down against the wood slice and make a knot next to the bead. Knot together the ends of the twine.

To attach the acorns and pinecones, cut a 4" length of twine. Thread a length of twine through the bottom hole of each wood slice. Thread an acorn or pinecone onto the twine and knot together the ends of the twine. Hot-glue the knot to the back of the ornament.♥

Designed by Kristin Detrick

crafts stick. Cut a point at the top of each ski; curl the pointed ends so the crafts stick is on the back of each ski. Cross the skis in a narrow X-shape; hot-glue in place.

For the poles, cut two 4½" lengths from the bamboo skewers. From the silver metal, cut two ⅞"-diameter circles and two ½×1" strips for the handle grips. Use the hole punch to make a hole through the center of each metal circle. Push a metal circle on one end of each skewer length until ½" of skewer is below the circle. To hold the circle in place, apply a line of hot glue around the skewer underneath the circle. For a strap, fold a 3" length of leather lacing in half. Position the lacing ends at the top of the pole; wrap a small piece of 20-gauge wire around the ends and the pole. Wrap the ½×1" metal strip around the top of the pole, covering the wire. Repeat for the second strap.

Cross the poles and wrap the center of the evergreen branch around the poles. Glue the center of the poles to the center of the skis. For the hanging loop, cut a 10" length of wire. Fold the wire in half and wrap the ends around the skis underneath the evergreen.♥

Designed by Heidi Boyd

Birdhouse Ornaments
Shown on page 71.

YOU WILL NEED
For each ornament:
Papier-mâché birdhouse (*above right*)
9" length of leather lacing
Dried moss
Dried and colored seedpods
Glue gun and hotmelt adhesive
Crafts stick

INSTRUCTIONS
Remove the gold hanging loop from the papier-mâché birdhouse. Fold the leather lacing in half to form a loop. Glue the lacing ends to the top center of the roof.

Ski Ornament
Shown above.

YOU WILL NEED
Silver tooling foil with wooden stylus
2 narrow, wooden crafts sticks
Glue gun and hotmelt adhesive
Bamboo skewers
⅛" hole punch
2—3" lengths of leather lacing
20-gauge green wire
4" piece of artificial evergreen branch

INSTRUCTIONS
For the skis, cut two 1½×8" strips from the silver metal sheet. Center a crafts stick on each metal strip with one end of the stick ½" from an end of the strip. Fold the long edges of the metal strip over the stick. Use the flat edge of the stylus to flatten and smooth each fold and to crease the metal along the bottom end of the

Hot-glue thin strips of moss to the edges and the bottom of the bird-house. Hot-glue dried seedpods to cover the roof and colored seedpods to cover the walls. Hot-glue small pieces of moss between the seedpods to fill in the spaces, using a crafts stick to push the moss down between the pods. For the perch, glue a bright stem or seedpod below the opening.♥

Designed by Heidi Boyd

Decoupage Fishing Frames
Shown on page 71.

YOU WILL NEED
Papier-mâché frame
Map-theme scrapbook paper
Stickers, such as leaves, fish, and fishing gear
Mod Podge decoupage medium
Sponge brush
Photo
Small brass leaf charm
Hemp cord
Glue gun and hotmelt adhesive

INSTRUCTIONS
On the front of the frame, measure from the picture opening to the outer edge of the frame; add ½". Using this measurement, cut two strips from the scrapbook paper 1" longer than the width of the frame and two strips 1" longer than the height of the frame.

Use the sponge brush to apply Mod Podge medium to the wrong side of the paper strips. Place two strips on opposite sides of the frame front, aligning a long edge of each strip with the picture opening.

Smooth the strips in place and fold the excess paper to the frame back, covering the edges. Place the two remaining strips on the frame front in the same manner. Position the stickers on the frame front. If necessary, wrap the stickers around the edges and to the back of the frame. Cut a piece of scrapbook paper to cover the frame back. Brush Mod Podge medium on the wrong side of the paper and center on the back of the frame; smooth in place. Apply an even coat of Mod Podge medium to the front of the frame, taking care to completely cover the edges of the stickers.

When completely dry, insert a photo. Cut a 5" length of hemp cord. Thread a leaf charm onto the hemp cord. Fold the hemp cord in half to form a loop; tie an overhand knot at the ends. Glue the knot to the top center of the frame.♥

Designed by Heidi Boyd

Acorn and Pinecone Garland

Shown at right.

YOU WILL NEED

19 pinecones
18 acorns
Aluminum foil
Baking sheet
Drill; $\frac{1}{16}$" drill bit
37—size 4 screw eyes
Pliers
Aleene's All Purpose Primer
Small paintbrushes
Bronze acrylic paint
Small stencil sponge
Ultra-fine gold glitter
17-foot length of jute twine
Tape
36 assorted color transparent glass crow beads

INSTRUCTIONS

Place the acorns and pinecones on an aluminum foil-lined baking sheet; bake in a 325° oven for 20 minutes. When the acorns and pinecones are cool, use the $\frac{1}{16}$" drill bit to make a hole at the center top of each piece. For the acorns, drill a hole through the cap and just into the shell. For the pinecones, drill a $\frac{1}{4}$" deep hole in the stem end. Insert a screw eye into each hole, using pliers if needed.

Use the paintbrush to coat the screw eyes with primer; let them dry. Paint each screw eye bronze with the stencil sponge. When the screw eyes are dry, sponge bronze paint onto an acorn or pinecone. Immediately sprinkle glitter lightly over the wet paint; let dry. Use a paintbrush to remove excess glitter. Continue to sponge paint and apply glitter to the acorns and pinecones one at a time.

Make a knot at one end of the twine and 1" away. Wrap tape around the opposite end of the twine. Thread a bead onto the taped end of the twine and slide it down to rest against the second knot. Make a knot next to the bead to hold it in place. Make a knot 1" away and thread an acorn onto the twine. Slide the acorn down to rest against the knot and make a knot next to the acorn to hold it in place. Next attach a bead, and then a pinecone in this same manner. Continue the bead, acorn, bead, pinecone pattern until you reach the end of the twine. Knot the end of the garland.♥

Designed by Kristin Detrick

Acorn Ornaments

Shown above.

YOU WILL NEED

Thin-wale corduroy fabric: ¼ yard each
   of mustard, rust, and moss green
⅛ yard of shimmery sheer fabric
   *(The designer chose fabric with a
   stitched grid)*
Elmer's Spray Adhesive glue
Glue gun and hotmelt adhesive
Natural oak leaves
Water-erasable fabric marker
Wire cutters

For each ornament:
2 floral wire stems
1—1½"-diameter wooden apple
1 skein of brown embroidery floss
11" length of gold cord

INSTRUCTIONS

Fold one color of corduroy in half
lengthwise and right sides together;
finger-crease along the fold. Lift up
the top half of the fabric and apply a
coat of spray adhesive to one-half of
the fabric. For the center vein of a leaf,
place a floral wire stem on one-half
of the fabric with one end just below

the fold and the opposite end
extending beyond a cut edge of the
fabric. Quickly place more stems,
5" apart, down the length of the fabric.
Fold down the top half of the fabric,
enclosing one end of the stems
between the fabric layers. Repeat
with the remaining two colors of
corduroy fabric.

For each acorn, wrap an entire skein
of embroidery floss around a wooden
apple, applying small dots of hot glue
to the top and bottom of the apple
as you're working to prevent the floss
from slipping.

For each acorn top, cut a 4" square
of sheer fabric. Fold in all four corners
of the fabric to meet at the center of
the square; then fold in all four of the
new corners to meet at the center of
the square. Glue the folded square,
smooth side up, to the center top of
the acorn.

Place a natural oak leaf over the
corduroy fabric with the top of the
leaf at the raw edge of the fabric and
lining up the center vein of the leaf
with an enclosed wire. Trace around
the leaf with the water-erasable fabric
marker. Cut out the leaf. Repeat to

cut two leaves for each ornament.
Twist the floral stems of two different
colored leaves together. Trim excess
wire and hot-glue the ends of the
leaves to the center top of the acorn.

For the hanging loop, thread one
end of the gold cord through the
twisted end of the leaves; knot the
cord ends together.♥
                    Designed by Heidi Boyd

Fishing Basket Ornaments
Shown below and on page 72.

YOU WILL NEED

For each ornament:
Miniature basket
3 Kreative Foam fish
Delta Ceramcoat Acrylic Paints: Avocado
   2006, Caucasian Flesh 2029, Straw
   2078, Medium Foliage Green 2536,
   and Sea Grass 2549
Delta Gleams paint: Metallic Kim Gold 2602
Wedge-shaped cosmetic sponges
Fine-tip permanent black marking pen
6½" length of ³⁄₁₆"-diameter wooden dowel
Miniature wooden spool
Beads: 1 wooden bead with a hole large
   enough to accommodate the dowel;
   2 small glass beads
Glue gun and hotmelt adhesive
24-gauge green or gold wire
Wire cutters
4" or 10" length of leather lacing

INSTRUCTIONS

Squeeze small pools of the acrylic paints onto a disposable plate. Dip a corner of a sponge into one of the green paints and lightly dab the paint over all surfaces of the fish, avoiding the eye. Lightly sponge the remaining two greens over the first color. Add Caucasian Flesh or Straw to the fins and edges of the fish. When the paint is dry, sponge a light coat of Metallic Kim Gold over the entire fish. Use the fine-tip permanent black marking pen to color the eye, draw the mouth, and define some of the fins.

For the fishing rod, slide the wooden bead and the spool onto one end of the dowel. Glue in place with the spool about 5/8" from the end. Wrap wire around the spool and then around the top end of the fishing rod. Cut the wire about 5" from the rod. Thread two glass beads onto the wire end. Bend a hook shape into the end of the wire and twist the wire slightly above and below the beads.

Arrange the fish and fishing rod in the basket; glue them securely in place. Tie a 4" length of leather lacing around the handle or a 10" length around the basket.♥

Designed by Heidi Boyd

Cedar Lodge Wreath
Shown at right.

YOU WILL NEED

12" straw wreath
6—14" lengths of 1/2"-diameter branches
Leather lacing
Sphagnum moss
Pinecones, dried seedpods, strawflowers, sweet Annie, and red celosia
Glue gun and hotmelt adhesive

INSTRUCTIONS

Arrange the branches around the outside edge on the back of the wreath with the branches crossing over each other. Hot-glue the center of each branch to the back edge of the wreath. Wrap leather lacing around the branches at the point where they cross; knot the lacing.

Separate the moss into small pieces. Hot-glue a thin layer of moss to the entire front of the wreath; it is not necessary to completely cover the straw. Begin with the moss at the branches and continue to cover the front of the wreath, stopping at the bottom inner edge at the center.

Decorate the wreath in complete rings of materials, starting at the outside and working toward the center. Hot-glue a ring of dried seed pods to the sides of the wreath just above the branches. Next, hot-glue a ring of pinecones around the top of the wreath. Hot-glue dried straw-flowers between the pinecones and the first ring of seed pods, filling in any spaces. Add a second ring of seedpods inside the pinecone ring; then add an inner ring of red dried celosia. Add a final inner ring of dried flowers or seedpods.♥

Designed by Heidi Boyd

Woodland Magic

Tiptoe through this once-upon-a-time wonderland of bejeweled dragonflies, velvet butterflies, and stardust—where seashells and peat-potted gnomes bloom, frog princes reign, and wood sprites pop up in the most surprising places. Teeming with childhood fairy tales and dreams, this captivating collection reaches to the secret places of the imagination, reaffirming the happily-ever-after magic that is Christmas.

A prince of an ornament, if ever there was, *above*. Assembled from ready-made objects, this little froggie leaps to the tree in the blink of an eye. You simply attach a purchased tiny plush toy to a silk water lily pad, then adorn him with a gold-trim crown and fur collar. Ladybug buttons keep him royal company.

Ever the proper gent, this stitch-and-stuff bullfrog, *opposite,* punctuates his camouflage vest and jacket with a most striking coral cravat. See how he looks at his world through snail-shell eyes? Give him as a gift or let him hop to the top of a fairy-tale tree.

Let's not forget Santa's helpers—those little elves who help work Christmas magic. With a swirl of fun, this oversize elfin Christmas stocking, *opposite,* sets up bold, suede-cloth stripes against a richly patterned tapestry boot. Capped in rich purple fur, it's well-heeled, too, sporting an anklet of velvet leaves and tiny jingle bells.

Smaller versions, *above,* are perfect to hug the branches of the tree. Stitched from striped fabric and golden velveteen, they're ringed with velvet foliage just like the larger stocking, and trimmed with a pinch of colorful beaded fringe.

Fairies, butterflies, and fanciful dragonflies take a lighthearted romp among the leaves so green. Beneath all the wreathed finery, *above*, runs a ring of silk juniper. Build on its natural beauty by adding ivy garlands, silk birds and butterflies, peach poinsettia leaves, plum balls, bead sprays, and velvet leaves. To finish the wreath, attach a few ornaments from the woodland tree, *opposite* and on *page 80*.

Clockwise from the top of the wreath shown *above,* the trims include a dragonfly, girl fairy, butterfly, boy fairy, pansy bouquet in a sea shell, and flower girl. Or make your selections from the woodland gathering, *opposite*.

Girl Fairy

Spherical Vellum Star

Beaded Icicle

Gnome

Flower Girl

All designs were created by Mary Jo Hiney.

Gnome Ornament

Shown on pages 81 and 87.

YOU WILL NEED

Waxed paper
Sculpey III polymer clay: gold
Rolling pin
1½"-diameter Styrofoam ball
12" length of ³⁄₁₆"-diameter wooden dowel
Aluminum foil
Baking sheet
Acrylic paint: brown, copper, coral,
    olive-green, and white
¼" stencil brush
Liner paintbrush
1" wooden bead
Tacky glue
Curly blond doll hair
Spanish moss
4 moss-green fabric leaves
¾ yard of 4mm olive-green ribbon
Size 3 embroidery needle
4—9mm-diameter bells
Glue gun and hotmelt adhesive
Wired acorns
Mushroom stamens
Small bird, snail shell, or bee
½ yard of ¾"-wide burgundy-and-gold
    ribbon
½ yard of ⅛"-wide gold metallic cording

INSTRUCTIONS

Cover your work area with a sheet of waxed paper. Knead the clay between the palms of your hands until it is soft and pliable. Use a craft-designated rolling pin to roll out the clay until it is ⅛" thick. Wrap the clay around the Styrofoam ball, smoothing the overlapping area flat.

For the nose, form a small piece of clay into a triangle. Center the triangle on one side of the ball and smooth it in place. Use a needle or end of a brush to puncture holes for the nostrils. Roll a long ⅛"-diameter snake. For the eyebrows, cut a 1¼" length from the snake; center it above the nose, slightly curving down the ends. Position two small ovals below the eyebrows and shape into eyes. From the snake, cut a 1¼" length for the top lip and 1½" length for the bottom lip. Shape the lips centered below the nose and smooth in place. Press two small ovals on the face for the cheeks. Shape a small oval into the chin. Shape two pointed ears on the sides of the head.

Push one end of the dowel into the center bottom of the head, forming a hole. Remove the dowel. Place the head on a baking sheet covered with aluminum foil. Put the baking sheet in the oven and bake the head according to the instructions on the clay package.

When the head is cool to the touch, use copper paint and the ¼" stencil brush to paint the forehead, eyebrows, cheeks, lips, ears, and chin. Lightly brush coral paint onto the cheeks. Use the liner paintbrush to paint the eyes white with brown irises.

Apply two coats of coral paint to the dowel and two coats of olive-green paint to the wooden ball, letting the paint dry between coats. When the paint is dry, glue the ball to one end of the dowel.

Cut a length of curly hair to encircle the head. Pull the hair apart so it is messy. Glue the hair around the head with tacky glue, leaving a bald spot. Glue Spanish moss over the bald spot.

For the collar, fold under ½" of each leaf to the wrong side at the wide end; glue in place. Visualizing a clock face, position the leaves with the tips pointing to 12, 3, 6, and 9. Overlap the wide ends at the center, leaving an opening large enough to accommodate the dowel; glue the leaves together. To attach the bells, cut four 6" lengths of 4mm olive-green ribbon. Use a ribbon length and a needle to sew a bell to the tip of each leaf. Knot the ribbon ends together three times and trim off the excess ribbon. Hot-glue the right side of the collar to the bottom of the head, centering the collar opening over the hole.

Twist the wired acorns and the mushroom stamens together, creating a 2"-diameter wreath. Hot-glue the wreath to the top of the head. Glue a small bird, snail shell, or bee to the top of the head.

Cut two 9" lengths of ¾"-wide burgundy-and-gold ribbon. Form each length into a bow, overlapping the ends at the center. Sew the ends together at the center, gathering the ribbon. Glue the dowel in the hole at the center bottom of the head. Hot-glue a bow to the front and the back of the dowel, underneath the leaf collar. Tie a bow at the center of the gold cording. Glue the bow to the center front of the dowel underneath the leaf collar. Tie a knot at each end of the cording. ♥

Frog Prince on Lily Pad

Shown opposite and on page 82.

YOU WILL NEED

5"-diameter silk water lily leaf
Clear glitter paint
Paintbrush
½ yard of ½"-wide antique gold
    metallic trim
Glue gun and hotmelt adhesive
Small, hunter-green plush frog
Beads: 8—6mm olive antique style
    octagonals and 7—8/0 olive hex
    cut seeds
Size 3 embroidery needle
Dark green sewing thread
1×7" strip of plum fake fur
2 ladybug buttons
Hunter-green embroidery floss

INSTRUCTIONS

Paint the dew on the water lily leaf with the clear glitter paint. Set the leaf aside to dry.

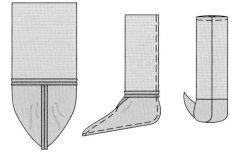

For the crown, roll the ½"-wide antique gold metallic trim into a tight coil; hot-glue to secure shape. Hot-glue the crown to the frog's head. Beginning at the center back, sew the beads to the head around the base of the crown, alternating the beads.

Fold the fake fur under ¼" on the top long edge; hot-glue in place. Wrap and glue the fur around the frog's neck with the folded edge at the top. Fluff the fur. Use embroidery floss to sew a ladybug button to one of the frog's hands. Use the floss to sew the leaf to the frog and the remaining ladybug button to the center front of the leaf.♥

A Proper English Frog
Shown on page 83.

YOU WILL NEED
Graph paper
⅓ yard of hunter-green suede cloth
¼ yard of olive-and-tan striped fabric
⅛ yard of tapestry fabric
⅓ yard of avocado-green tiger-print plush fake fur
¼ yard of leopard-print plush fake fur
3×22" strip of coral silk shimmer organza
Matching sewing thread
Polyester fiberfill
2 snail shells
Krazy Glue adhesive
Tacky glue
5" length of 20-gauge green cotton-wrapped wire

Hunter-green embroidery floss
3" miniature eyeglasses
Pewter buttons: 3 acorns and 1 squirrel

INSTRUCTIONS
Enlarge the pattern pieces, *page 90,* on graph paper. Cut out the pattern pieces. Sew all pieces with right sides together using ¼" seam allowances, unless otherwise noted.

Cut the Fabrics
From the hunter-green suede cloth, cut:
• 2 frog body fronts, 2 frog body backs, 2 pant fronts, 2 pant backs, 4 arms, and 2—1⅛×8" strips for the eyes
From the olive-and-tan stripe fabric, cut:
• 2 legs
From the tapestry fabric, cut:
• 4 feet
From the tiger-print fabric, cut:
• 2 coat fronts, 1 coat back, 2 sleeves, and 2 front jacket facings
From the leopard-print fabric, cut:
• 2 vest fronts and 1 vest back

Sew the Frog
Pin together the feet in pairs and sew the center front seams only as shown at *right*. Press the seam allowances open. Referring to the

diagrams *above,* sew the feet to the legs at the ankle. Press the seam allowances toward the legs. Align the long edges of each leg and the bottom edges of the feet, matching the ankle seams; sew together, leaving the top edges of the legs open. Trim the seams, clip the curves, and turn the legs right side out. Stuff the legs with polyester fiberfill, stopping 1" from the top edges. Sew the openings closed, centering the seam on the center back of the leg.

Sew the arms together in pairs, using a very short stitch length at the fingers and leaving the top edge open. Trim the seams, clip the curves, and clip to the dots indicated on the pattern. Turn the arms right side out. Stuff the arms with fiberfill, stopping 1" from the top edges. Sew the openings closed.

For the mouth, sew the dart on each frog front. Sew the frog body fronts together at the center front seam, matching the dart seam. Clip the curves and press the seam allowance open. Sew the frog body backs together at the center back, leaving an opening for stuffing as indicated on the pattern; press the seam allowances open.

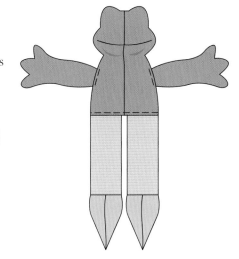

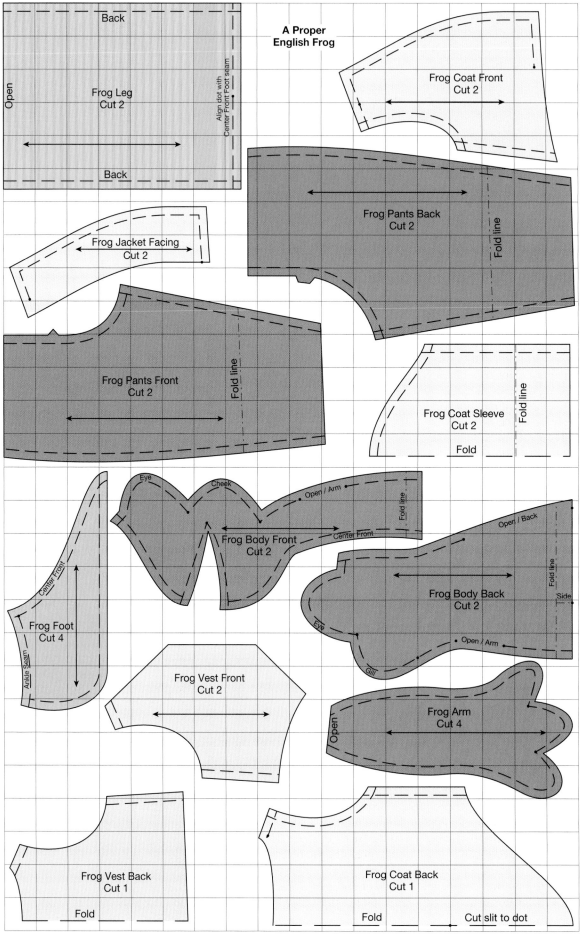

A Proper English Frog

Back

Open

Frog Leg
Cut 2

Align dot with
Center Front Foot seam

Back

Frog Coat Front
Cut 2

Frog Jacket Facing
Cut 2

Frog Pants Back
Cut 2

Fold line

Frog Pants Front
Cut 2

Fold line

Frog Coat Sleeve
Cut 2

Fold line

Fold

Eye

Cheek

Open / Arm

Fold line

Frog Body Front
Cut 2

Center Front

Open / Back

Frog Body Back
Cut 2

Fold line

Side

Eye

Open / Arm

Gill

Center Front

Frog Foot
Cut 4

Ankle Seam

Frog Vest Front
Cut 2

Open

Frog Arm
Cut 4

Frog Vest Back
Cut 1

Fold

Frog Coat Back
Cut 1

Fold

Cut slit to dot

90

1 Square = 1 Inch

Sew the frog front to the frog back, easing the eye and cheek areas to fit and leaving the bottom edge open and the side openings for the arms as indicated on the patterns. Clip the curves, press the seam allowances open, and turn the body right side out.

Press under ½" at the bottom open edges of the body. Pin the legs centered in the bottom body opening; sew the bottom opening closed, catching the legs firmly in the stitching. Turn under ¼" at the side openings for the arms. Pin an arm in each opening. Sew the openings closed, catching the arms firmly in the stitching. Stuff the body through the center back opening. Slip-stitch the back opening closed.

For the eyes, glue the snail shells to the frog's face with adhesive. Let the adhesive dry. Press under ¼" on the long edges of the 1⅛×8" hunter-green strips; glue in place with glue. Fold the strips in half again lengthwise, aligning the pressed edges and enclosing the raw edges; glue in place. Straighten one short edge of each strip. Beginning with the straight edge at the bottom outer edge of a snail shell, glue one side of a strip over the entire eye seam. Trim off the excess strip at the bottom outer edge of the second snail shell. Glue the second strip along the bottom of the snail shells, beginning and ending with the first strip.

For the mouth, center the green cotton-wrapped wire over the mouth seam; curl up the wire ends. Use

hunter-green embroidery floss to sew the wire to the face. Place the glasses on the frog. Sew the glasses to the sides of the frog's head.

Dress the Frog

Sew together the pant backs at the center back and the pants fronts at the center front; press the seam allowances open. Sew the pants front to the back at the sides and inseam, as shown *below*. Press the seam allowances open. To hem, turn each pant leg under as indicated on the pattern; tack in place at the seams. Press under ½" at the top edge of the pants. Hand-sew running stitches close to the pressed edge. Slip the pants on the frog. Pull the thread ends to fit the pants snugly around the frog's waist; knot the thread to secure.

Sew the vest back to the vest fronts along the shoulder and sides. Press the seam allowances open. Press under ¼" on all raw edges of the vest; sew close to the pressed edges. Slip the vest on the frog. Overlap the center front edges of the vest; sew together with an acorn and a squirrel button.

Sew the coat fronts to the coat back at the shoulder seams, beginning at the sleeve edge and stopping at the dot indicated on the coat front pattern. Press the seam allowances open. Sew the sleeves to the armhole openings of the coat. Press the seam allowances toward the sleeves. Sew the coat front to the back along the side and under-arm; press the seam allowances open. To hem, turn up 1" at the bottom edge of each sleeve; tack in place at the underarm seam.

Sew a front facing to each coat front at the bottom, front, and shoulder edges, stopping and starting at the dots. Trim the corners and clip the curves. Turn the facing right side out and press. Press under ¼" at the remaining neck edge and at the bottom edges of the coat, including the center back slit. Sew close to the pressed edges. Slip-stitch the raw edges of the front facings to the inside of the coat.

Wrap the organza around the frog's neck and tie the ends into a square knot. Tuck the ends under the vest front. Slip the coat on the frog. Sew an acorn button to each foot at the ankle seam.♥

Elf Shoe Ornament

Shown below and on page 85.

YOU WILL NEED

Tracing paper
9" square of gold velveteen fabric
Matching sewing threads
Turning tool, such as dowel, safety pin, or pencil
Chenille stem
Glue gun and hotmelt adhesive
Polyester fiberfill
6" length of 4mm olive-green silk ribbon
Size 3 embroidery needle
1—9mm gold bell
3"-long sewing needle
Gold sewing thread
5 olive-green velvet leaves
9" length of narrow gold cording
7×6" piece of olive-and-tan striped fabric
2" length of 1½"-wide beaded fringe

INSTRUCTIONS

Trace the shoe pattern, *page 92,* onto tracing paper. Cut out the pattern piece. Use the pattern to cut two shoes

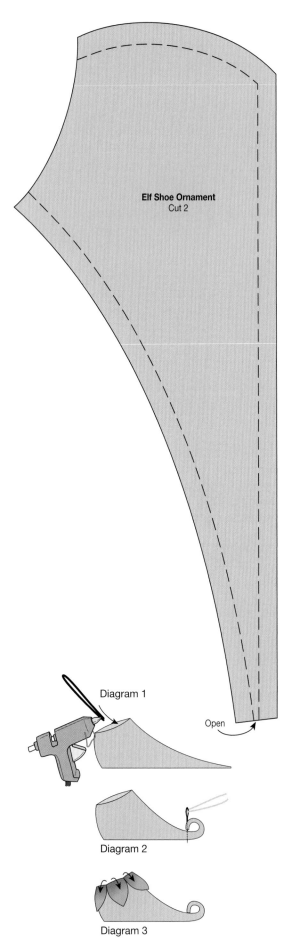

Elf Shoe Ornament
Cut 2

Diagram 1

Open

Diagram 2

Diagram 3

Woodland Magic

from the gold velveteen. Sew all pieces with right sides together, using ¼" seam allowances unless otherwise noted.

Pin together the shoes and sew the back and bottom edges. Press the seam allowances open. Sew the top seam, leaving the toe and ankle edges open. Press the top seam allowances open. Clip the curves and turn the shoe right side out, using a turning tool to pull out the toe area of the shoe. Press under ½" at the top open edge of the shoe; sew close to the pressed edges. Fold the chenille stem in half. Place a dab of hotmelt adhesive on the ends of the chenille stem. Immediately insert the folded chenille stem through the shoe, placing the glued end at the toe, as shown in Diagram 1 *below*. Lightly stuff the toe area of the shoe with polyester fiberfill and firmly fill the rest of the shoe.

Thread a needle with the 4mm ribbon. Use the ribbon to sew the bell to the toe of the shoe. Knot the ribbon ends together three times and trim off the excess ribbon. Roll the toe into a spiral, shaping the chenille stem. Use the long sewing needle and sewing thread to sew the toe to the shoe, inserting the needle through the shoe to the bottom seam and then back up to the top seam, as shown in Diagram 2 *below*. Repeat and knot the thread.

Hot-glue the top edge of five velvet leaves to the inside of the shoe at the open edge, overlapping the leaves as needed. Fold the leaves down over the outside of the shoe, as shown in Diagram 3 *below*. For the hanging loop, fold the narrow gold cording in half. Glue the ends to the inside center back of the shoe.

Fold the 7×6" stocking piece in half to measure 3½×6". Sew the edges together, leaving one short edge open for the top of the stocking. Press the seam allowances open. Turn the stocking right side out. To form the cuff, fold 1¾" to the inside and then fold 1" to the outside; press. Hot-glue

the stocking bottom to the inside of the shoe at the ankle, covering the fiberfill.

Fold the ends of the beaded fringe tape to meet at the center back of the tape. Hand-sew running stitches through the tape and pull the thread as tight as possible; knot the thread. Glue the gathered tape to the center front of the shoe at the ankle.♥

Woodland Magic Wreath
Shown on page 86.

YOU WILL NEED
18" artificial juniper wreath
2—6-foot-long dew-dripped ivy garlands
26-gauge florist wire
Wire cutters
2 dusty-peach silk poinsettias
Glue gun and hotmelt adhesive
Woodland Magic ornaments (*pages 96–103*): Girl Fairy, Boy Fairy, Dragonfly, Butterfly, Flower Girl, and Sea Shell Pansy
Purchased small bird and butterfly
Nylon fishing line
2 burgundy velvet leaf sprays
3 crystal bead sprays
12—1" frosted or shiny plum glass bulbs

INSTRUCTIONS
Tightly wrap and wire one of the ivy garlands one time around the outer edge of the juniper wreath. Bring the excess of this garland into the body of the wreath, wiring it in place. Use as much of the second ivy garland as needed to complete the wreath, wiring the garland in place.

Take apart the silk poinsettias in layers. Tuck the poinsettia layers in the juniper and ivy; hot-glue in place. Arrange the Woodland Magic ornaments and the purchased small bird and butterfly on the wreath. When pleased with the arrangement, wire the ornaments in place or tie them to the wreath with nylon fishing line.

Take apart the velvet leaf sprays and crystal bead sprays. Wire the leaves, bead sprays, and glass bulbs around the wreath, filling in any open spaces.

Woodland Magic Stocking
Shown on page 84 and below.

YOU WILL NEED
Graph paper
³/₈ yard of tapestry fabric
¼ yard of rust suede cloth
⅛ yard of plum suede cloth
¼ yard of long-haired plum fake fur
½ yard of lining fabric
7 burgundy velvet leaves
Matching sewing thread
Turning tool, such as a dowel, safety pin, or pencil
2 chenille stems
Glue gun and hotmelt adhesive
Polyester stuffing
4mm olive-green silk ribbon
Size 3 embroidery needle
Bells: 6—12mm and 2—9mm
3"-long sewing needle

INSTRUCTIONS
Enlarge the stocking patterns on *page 94* onto graph paper. Cut out the pattern pieces. Sew all pieces with right sides together, using ¼" seam allowances unless otherwise noted.

Cut the Fabrics
From the tapestry fabric, cut:
• 2 stocking feet
From the rust suede cloth, cut:
• 3—1⅞×20" strips and 1—5½×20" strip
From the plum suede cloth, cut:
• 4—1⅞×20" strips and 1—2×6" strip for the hanging loop
From the plum fake fur, cut:
• 1—9×18" rectangle for the cuff
From the lining fabric, cut:
• 2 stocking pieces

Sew the Stocking
Beginning and ending with plum strips, sew the long edges of the 1⅞"-wide plum and rust suede cloth strips together. Sew the 5½×20" rust strip to one of the plum strips. Press all of the seam allowances open.

With right sides facing, fold the assembled striped fabric in half, aligning the seams. Pin the sock pattern on the folded fabric with the bottom edge of the pattern aligned with the raw edge of the bottom plum stripe; cut out two stocking tops.

Sew the stocking tops together at the center back seam, matching the stripes. Press the seam allowances open. Sew the feet together at the heel and bottom edge. Press the seam allowances open.

Pin a velvet leaf to the right side of the foot, centering the leaf over the heel seam with the wide end of the leaf about ½" above the top edge of the fabric. Pin three leaves to both the front and back stocking feet in the same manner, overlapping the leaves about ¼" and angling them to point toward the toe. Baste the leaves in place. Sew the stocking top to the stocking bottom, catching the leaves in the stitching. Press the seam allowances toward the stocking top.

Sew the center front edges together, matching the stripes and leaving the top of the foot open. Press the seam allowance open as much as possible. Clip the curves and turn the stocking right side out, using a turning tool to pull the toe area out of the stocking.

Turn ½" to the inside at the open foot edge. Hot-glue the ends of two chenille stems together. Place a dab of hotmelt adhesive on the end of the stems. Immediately insert the stems through the stocking, placing the glued end at the toe. Squeeze the open edges together, adhering the chenille stem in place and gluing the fabric edges together. Use polyester fiberfill to lightly stuff the stocking bottom from the toe to about 7" from the toe, pushing the chenille stems against the center front seam.

Sew the lining pieces together, leaving the top edge open. Trim the seams and clip the curves; do not turn. Slip the lining inside the stocking with wrong sides together. Baste the top edges of the stocking and lining together.

For the hanging loop, press under ½" on each long edge of the 2×6" plum strip. Fold the strip in half lengthwise, aligning the pressed edges; press again. Sew the long edge opposite the fold together. Fold the strip in half, forming a loop. Baste the ends to the top inside corner on the heel side of the stocking with the loop side down.

For the cuff, sew the short edges together with a ½" seam allowance, pushing the fur away from the seam while sewing. Finger-press or use a cool iron to press the seam allowances open. Fold the bottom edge of the cuff up 3" to the wrong side. Hand-sew or glue the raw edge in place.

Slip the cuff inside the stocking with the right side of the cuff facing the wrong side of the stocking and aligning the cuff seam with the center back seam of the stocking. Sew the top edges together with a ½" seam allowance. Pull the cuff away from

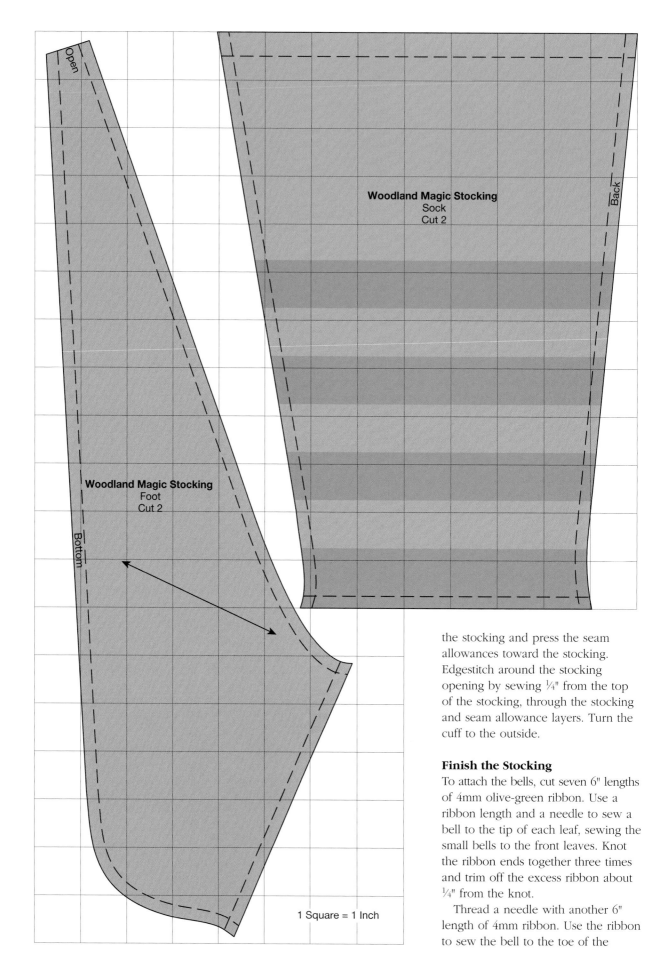

Woodland Magic Stocking
Sock
Cut 2

Open

Back

Woodland Magic Stocking
Foot
Cut 2

Bottom

1 Square = 1 Inch

the stocking and press the seam
allowances toward the stocking.
Edgestitch around the stocking
opening by sewing ¼" from the top
of the stocking, through the stocking
and seam allowance layers. Turn the
cuff to the outside.

Finish the Stocking
To attach the bells, cut seven 6" lengths
of 4mm olive-green ribbon. Use a
ribbon length and a needle to sew a
bell to the tip of each leaf, sewing the
small bells to the front leaves. Knot
the ribbon ends together three times
and trim off the excess ribbon about
¼" from the knot.

Thread a needle with another 6"
length of 4mm ribbon. Use the ribbon
to sew the bell to the toe of the

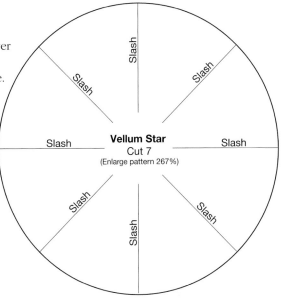

Vellum Star
Cut 7
(Enlarge pattern 267%)

Slash

stocking in the same manner. Roll the toe into a spiral, shaping the chenille stems. Use the long sewing needle and sewing thread to sew the toe in place, inserting the needle through the stocking to the bottom seam and then back up to the top seam. Repeat and knot the thread.♥

Beaded Icicle Ornament

Shown on page 87.

YOU WILL NEED

15" length of 24-gauge gold wire
Needle-nose pliers
4 each of 7 different specialty beads in shades of lavender, plum, and mauve
Seed beads: silver size 11/0 triangle and plum metallic size 11/0
Wire cutters

INSTRUCTIONS

Wrap one wire end three times around the tip of the needle-nose pliers. Flatten the wire end with the pliers. Referring to the diagram *below*, begin threading beads onto the wire, with the smaller specialty beads, thread the beads onto the wire, alternating a seed bead with a specialty bead until the beaded area measures 8" to 10".

Not actual size

For the top loop, thread 20 silver seed beads on the wire. Shape the silver-beaded area into a circle. Tightly wrap the wire three times around the bottom of the circle. Trim away the excess wire with the wire cutters.

Wrap the beaded wire around your index finger. Pull down on the wraps to loosen the coil.♥

Vellum Star

Shown below and on page 87.

YOU WILL NEED

8½×11" sheets of vellum paper:
    3 frosted with swirls,
    2 pale pink, and 2 pale blue
Tacky glue
¾ yard of 4mm white silk ribbon
3" to 5"-long sewing needle
Beads: 3 aqua leaves, 3 yellow butterflies, 6 rose flat rounds, and 15—8/0 hex-cut seeds
Size 3 embroidery needle
1 yard of 1"-wide mauve velvet ribbon
Glue gun and hotmelt adhesive
Gold star glitter
Spray adhesive

INSTRUCTIONS

Enlarge the pattern *above*, using a copy machine. Cut out the pattern piece. Use the pattern piece to cut one from each sheet of vellum paper. Cut the slashes in each vellum circle to make eight wedges as shown on the pattern.

To make a single star, bring in the outer corners of each wedge to overlap about ¼", creating eight small cones. Glue the overlapped edges together. Do not flatten the cones. Repeat with each vellum circle.

Beginning at the bottom, layer the stars with cones facing up, as follows: pink, frosted, blue, pink, frosted, blue, and frosted. Thread a 15" length of 4mm white ribbon through the long needle. Thread the needle and ribbon through the center of the layered stars

from top to bottom, leaving a ribbon tail at the top. Return the needle and ribbon to the top of the layers about ¼" from the first stitch. Repeat, crisscrossing the stitches at the center bottom of the star layers. Both ribbon ends should extend from the center top. Pull the ribbon ends to draw the star layers together.

Thread the remaining 4mm white ribbon through the embroidery needle; knot one end. Thread the leaf and butterfly beads onto the ribbon, alternating them with the flat round. Thread on the hex-cut seed beads. Starting at the center bottom, draw the ribbon through the layered stars. Knot the three ribbon ends together at the center top.

To attach the hanging loop, thread each ribbon end at the center top of

the star through a needle one at a time. Bring the needle through the center of the 1"-wide velvet ribbon with the velvet side toward the star. Knot the ribbon ends together again above the ribbon. Hot-glue the velvet ribbon to the star top for additional stability.

Apply a light coat of spray adhesive to the star. Immediately pour the glitter onto the sticky surface. Set the star aside to dry. Repeat for a more glittery appearance.♥

Flower Girl Ornament
Shown below.

YOU WILL NEED
1½"-tall porcelain fairy head with
  shoulder plate
Pale gold metallic acrylic paint
Paintbrush
Clear glitter
2 stems of velvet leaves, with 3 leaves
  on each stem
Tacky glue
1"-wide foam brush
1 velvet pansy
3½"-diameter lavender velvet/organza
  flower
Green florist's tape
5 soft-blue velvet and satin leaves
⅓ yard of 1"-wide metallic gold lace
Sewing needle
Gold thread
Glue gun and hotmelt adhesive

INSTRUCTIONS
Apply a light coat of pale gold metallic paint on the porcelain fairy head with the paintbrush. Use the foam brush to

apply glue to the velvet leaf stems. Immediately pour clear glitter over the wet glue, tap off the excess glitter, and set the leaves aside to dry. Glitter the velvet pansy in the same manner.

Remove the stamens from the 3½"-diameter lavender flower. Reserve the stamens for later. Position the velvet leaf sprays onto the stem of the lavender flower. Wire the stems together and wrap the stems with florist's tape.

Glue the blue velvet and satin leaves onto the shoulder plate of the fairy head. Overlap the ends of the metallic gold lace, forming a circle. Hand-sew running stitches along the top edge of the lace. Slip the lace circle around the neck of the fairy head with the overlap at the center back. Pull the thread ends so the lace gathers tightly around the neck; knot the thread.

Use hot glue and tacky glue to attach the back of the head and the shoulder plate to the center of the flower. Let the glue dry. Carefully glue the stamens between the chin and lace ruffle. Use hotmelt adhesive and tacky glue to glue the pansy to the top of the head.♥

Boy Fairy Ornament
Shown above right.

YOU WILL NEED
Tracing paper
Waxed paper
Sculpey III polymer clay: gold
Small foot and hand mold
Darning needle
Aluminum foil
Baking sheet
Acrylic paint: blue, coral, metallic gold,
  and white
Paintbrushes
5 chenille stems
¼ yard of plum cross-dyed velvet fabric
5" square of avocado-green tiger-print
  plush fur
Matching sewing thread
1 yard of ⅜"-wide antique gold-and-plum
  metallic trim

¼ yard of ⅜"-wide antique gold
  metallic trim
Tacky glue
18" length of 24-gauge gold wire
Beads: berry bugles, 11/0 plum metallic
  seeds, and 8/0 celadon hex-cut seeds
5 plum-and-green velvet leaves
Glue gun and hotmelt adhesive
1 wired mushroom stamen

INSTRUCTIONS
Trace the patterns *opposite* onto tracing paper. Cut out the pattern pieces. Sew all pieces with right sides together, using ¼" seam allowances unless otherwise noted.

Assemble the Body
Cover your work area with a sheet of waxed paper. Knead the clay between the palms of your hands until it is soft and pliable.

Roll a 1¼"-long egg-shaped oval of clay for the head; add a neck to the bottom, smoothing the edges. For the nose, form a small piece of clay into a triangle. Center the triangle on one side of the head and smooth it in place, shaping the nose. Use a needle to make the nostrils. Roll a very fine snake for the eyebrows; center it above the nose. Position two tiny ovals below the eyebrows and shape into eyes. Use pieces of a very fine snake to shape an open mouth centered below the nose; smooth in place. Shape a tiny oval into the chin. Shape two pointed ears on the sides of the head. Use the darning needle to make a hole through the neck from side to side.

Use the molds to make two feet and two hands. Use the darning needle to make a hole through each foot and hand from side to side.

Place the head, feet, and hands on a baking sheet covered with aluminum foil. Put the baking sheet in the oven and bake the pieces according to the instructions on the clay package.

When the clay pieces are cool to the touch, brush metallic gold paint on all the clay surfaces. Lightly brush coral paint on the cheeks and lips. Paint the eyes white with blue irises.

For the arms, insert a chenille stem through the hole at the bottom of the neck. Adjust the stem so there is an equal amount on each side of the neck. Wrap the stem around the neck to secure. Thread each end of the arm chenille stem through the hole in a hand. Wrap the chenille stem around itself above the hand, adjusting the length of the stem for a 3½"-long arm length.

For the legs, attach a chenille stem to the shoulder area of the arm chenille stem on each side of the body. Thread the opposite end of each leg stem through a foot. Wrap the stem around itself above the foot, adjusting the length of the leg so the figure will be approximately 7" tall. Use a fourth chenille stem to weave together the two leg chenille stems in a figure-8 motion for about 2", starting below the head.

Dress the Fairy

Use the patterns *above* to cut two pants and one top from the plum velvet fabric, referring to the diagram

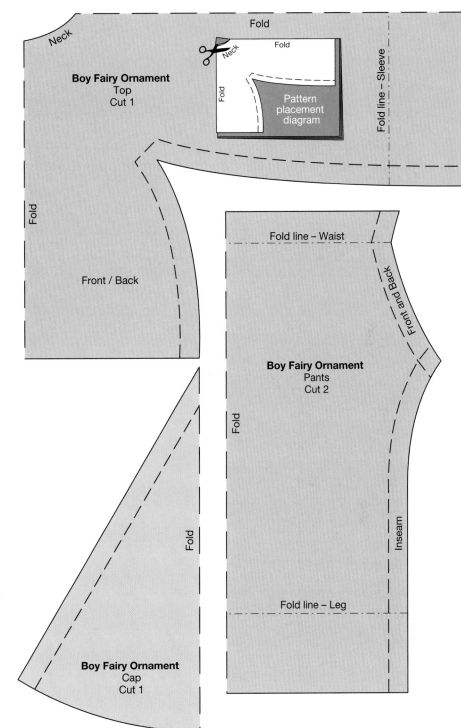

above for placement of the Top pattern on the folded fabric. Cut one cap from the tiger-print plush fur.

Sew the pants together at the center front and center back. Press the seam allowances open. Sew the inseams together, *right,* matching the center front and back seams. Press the seam allowances open and turn the pants right side out. To hem, turn up 1" at

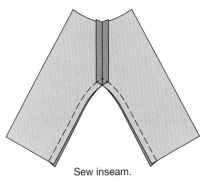

Sew inseam.

the bottom of each pant leg. Hand-sew running stitches ¾" from the bottom edge. Press under ⅜" at the top edge of the pants. Hand-sew running stitches close to the pressed edge. Slip the pants on the fairy. Pull the thread ends to fit the pants snugly around the waist of the chenille stem body; knot the thread to secure. Pull the thread ends to fit each pant leg snugly around the top of the foot; knot the thread to secure.

Sew the underarm and side seam of the shirt, as shown in the diagram *below*. Clip to the stitching at the underarm. Press the seam allowances open. Turn the shirt right side out.

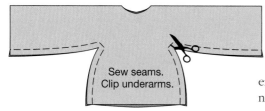

Sew seams.
Clip underarms.

Press under ¼" at the bottom edge of the shirt. Sew antique gold-and-plum trim on the right side of the shirt to secure the hem. Turn up a scant 1" at the bottom of each sleeve. Hand-sew running stitches ¾" from the bottom edge of each sleeve and 1¼" from the bottom edge of the shirt, leaving long thread ends. Slip the shirt on the fairy. Fold under the neck edge and hand-sew running stitches close to the folded edge. Pull the thread ends to gather the neckline tightly around the clay neck; knot the thread to secure. Pull the thread ends to fit each sleeve snugly around the top of the hand, knot the thread to secure. Pull the thread ends to gather the shirt around the waist; knot the thread to secure.

Wrap and glue antique gold-and-plum trim around the gathers on the pant legs and sleeves with tacky glue. Wrap and glue the antique gold trim around the gathers at the waist of the shirt.

For the wings, cut an 18" length of gold wire. Thread berry bugles, plum

metallic seeds, and celadon hex-cut seeds on the wire, alternating the bugle beads with the seed beads, until the beaded area measures about 10". With the beads centered on the wire, bring in the end beads to meet at the center, creating a bow-shape. Wrap each end of the wire several times around the center of the beaded area. To attach the wings, wrap the wire around the fairy's neck several times. Trim off the excess wire.

For the leaf collar, overlap the side edges of the velvet leaves slightly. Hand-sew running stitches about ¼" from one end of the velvet leaves, sewing the leaves together and joining the first leaf with the last. Slip the collar over the fairy's head, positioning one leaf at the center front, one on each shoulder, and two in the back. Pull the thread ends to fit the collar snugly to the neck, covering the wing wires.

Fold the cap in half and sew together the straight edges. Press the seam allowances open. Turn the cap right side out. Cut a 6" length of chenille stem; fold the stem in half. Hot-glue the ends to the inside tip of the cap. Turn the bottom edge of the cap under ½" and glue in place. Hot-glue the cap to the head. Glue the antique gold-and-plum trim around the cap with tacky glue. Wire the mushroom stamen around the tip of the cap and bend the chenille stem to shape the cap.♥

Sew cap seam.

Girl Fairy Ornament
Shown above.

YOU WILL NEED
Tracing paper
Porcelain fairy head with 1½"
  shoulder plate
Pale metallic gold acrylic paint
Paintbrush
¼ yard of lavender-print cotton fabric

Erasable fabric marker
Matching sewing thread
Turning tool, such as a wooden skewer
  or knitting needle
Polyester fiberfill
2 chenille stems
Needle-nose pliers
3–5"-long sewing needle
Tacky glue
Glue gun and hotmelt adhesive
Velvet leaves: 3—2" lavender and
  4—1" orchid
Clear glitter
3 yellow organza-and-satin flowers
18" length of 24-gauge gold wire
Beads: 12 yellow tulips, yellow-gold seeds,
  gold bugles, and 3 yellow butterflies
⅓ yard of 1½"-wide gold metallic ribbon
¼ yard of 1⅛"-wide gold metallic lace trim
¼ yard of ⅜"-wide antique gold
  metallic trim
3 mauve satin ribbon rosettes
⅓ yard of 4mm plum silk ribbon

INSTRUCTIONS
Trace the patterns *opposite* onto tracing paper. Cut out the pattern pieces.

Paint a light coat of pale metallic gold on the porcelain head and shoulder plate. Set the head aside to dry.

Sew the Body
On a doubled layer of lavender-print fabric, use the erasable fabric marker to trace one body, two arms, and two legs on the wrong side of the fabric,

leaving at least ½" between the tracings. Pin the fabric layers together in several places. Use a very short stitch length to sew on the traced lines, leaving openings as indicated on the pattern pieces. To sew the tiny curves, it may be necessary to sew individual stitches, repositioning the presser foot with each stitch. Cut out the body parts ⅛" beyond the sewn lines. Clip to the stitching line all around each shape, especially at inward and outward curves and at the leave-open marks. Carefully turn each piece right side out, using the flat end of a skewer. Use the skewer to gently push out the seams.

For a leg, use the skewer to push in tiny amounts of polyester fiberfill, firmly stuffing half of the foot. Cut a 4" length of chenille stem. Bend each end with a needle-nose pliers. Slip the stem into the leg and continue to stuff the leg firmly. Slip-stitch the opening closed. Repeat for the second leg.

For the arm, use the skewer to push in tiny amounts of polyester fiberfill to firmly stuff half of the hand. Cut a 3" length of chenille stem. Bend each end with a needle-nose pliers. Slip the stem into the arm and continue to stuff the arm firmly. Slip-stitch the opening closed. Repeat for the second arm. Stuff the body firmly with fiberfill; slip-stitch closed.

Thread the long needle with four lengths of thread. Knot the thread ends together. Place a leg on either side of the body at the hip area. Insert the needle through one leg, the body, and the second leg and return back through in the opposite direction. Repeat and knot the thread. Sew the arms to either side of the body at the shoulders in the same manner.

Pour tacky glue inside the shoulder plate area of the porcelain head. Squeeze hotmelt adhesive into the center of the shoulder plate. Place the head over the shoulders of the body. Let the glue dry for several hours.

Dress the Fairy
To make a double-sided leaf, glue together two of the lavender leaves with wrong sides facing. Working on one at a time, lightly coat both sides of the double-sided leaf, the remaining lavender leaf, and all the orchid leaves with tacky glue. Immediately sprinkle the wet glue with glitter, tap off the excess glitter, and set each piece aside to dry.

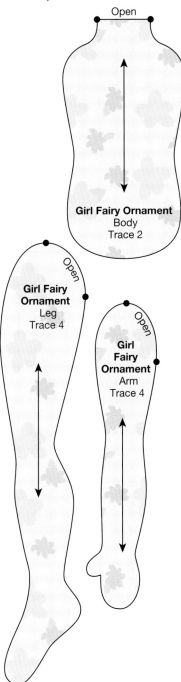

Open

Girl Fairy Ornament
Body
Trace 2

Open

Girl Fairy Ornament
Leg
Trace 4

Open

Girl Fairy Ornament
Arm
Trace 4

For the skirt, pull apart the yellow organza and satin flowers. Set aside two full petal layers for the head. Cut an opening at the center of the remaining petal layers large enough to slip over the body. Beginning at the hips, glue the petal layers to the body, spacing the layers about ⅛" apart and ending just above the waist.

For the wings, thread seven seed and seven bugle beads on the 18" length of wire, alternating the beads. Alternate and thread three tulips, narrow end first, and three bugles on the wire. Thread on 3 seeds for the center top of a wing. Alternate and thread on three bugles and three tulips, wide end first. Alternating the beads, thread on seven bugles and seven seeds. Repeat the beading pattern for the second wing. With the beads centered on the wire, bring in the end beads to meet at the center, creating a bow-shape. Wrap each end of the wire several times around the center of the beaded area. To attach the wings, wrap the wire ends around the fairy's body underneath the arms. Trim off the excess wire. Shape the loops into teardrop-shaped wings.

Beginning at the center back, crinkle and wrap the 1½"-wide metallic ribbon around the fairy's chest, covering the cut edge of the skirt and the wire. Glue the ribbon ends in place. Wrap and glue the 1⅛"-wide gold lace trim once around the chest, beginning and ending at the center back and having the top edge cover the bottom edge of the shoulder plate. Trim off the excess lace trim.

Glue an orchid leaf over each shoulder with tacky glue. Glue another orchid leaf along each shoulder, pointing toward the arm. Glue the double-sided lavender leaf to the center back of the body and the shoulder plate. Glue the remaining lavender leaf to the back about ½" below the top of the double-sided leaf.

Glue the ⅜"-wide metallic trim around the fairy's head for the wreath.

Woodland Magic

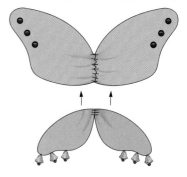

Working with the two set-aside petal layers, fold the layers in half and sew running stitches through the layers about ¾" from the outer edges. Pull the stitches as tightly as possible and wrap the thread several times around the pulled stitches. Knot the thread and trim away the excess petal layers ⅛" beyond the stitches. Use tacky glue to attach the underside of the gathered petal layers to the top of the head. Glue the ribbon rosettes to the top of the head.

To attach the butterfly beads to the feet, bring a threaded needle out at the center front of the ankle. Slip the needle through a butterfly bead, a seed bead, back through the butterfly bead, and into the foot; knot the thread. Tie a bow with the plum silk ribbon around the fairy's waist. Sew a butterfly bead and seed bead to the center of the bow in the same manner.♥

Butterfly Ornament
Shown above.

YOU WILL NEED
14-gauge soldering wire
Soldering gun and solder
Wire cutters
Tracing paper
8×12" piece of avocado-green velvet burnout fabric
6×8" piece of coral silk shimmer organza
Matching sewing threads
Size 5 embroidery needle
Beads: 2 rose flowers, 3—6mm×8mm burgundy oval crystals, 7—6mm plum pearls, 8 mauve tulips, size 11/0 magenta seeds, and dark rose bugles
24-gauge gold wire
Needle-nose pliers
Glue gun and hotmelt adhesive

INSTRUCTIONS
For the wings, bend 14-gauge soldering wire into a wing shape, beginning and ending at the inner point and referring to the wing diagrams *opposite*. Solder the wire together at the point and cut away the excess wire. Make two upper

wings and two lower wings. As an alternative to a soldering gun, wrap the soldering wire end around the starting point, cut the wire, flatten the wrap with a hammer, and hot-glue the ends together.

Trace the wing patterns *opposite* onto tracing paper. Cut out the pattern pieces. Use the patterns to cut two upper wings from the velvet and two lower wings from the organza. With right sides facing, sew each wing along the curved edges with a ¼" seam allowance, leaving the short straight edges open as indicated on the patterns. Turn each wing right side out.

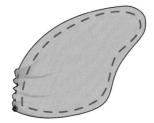

Press under ¼" on the open edges of an upper wing. Hand-sew running stitches along the pressed edges. Insert a wire upper wing into the fabric wing. Pull the thread ends to draw the fabric around the inner point of the wire wing. Knot the thread ends; trim off the excess. Repeat for each wing.

Sew the plum pearl beads to one of the upper wings at the dots marked on the pattern, running the thread between the fabric layers from dot to

dot. Bead the second upper wing in the same manner, reversing the direction of the wing for the opposite side of the butterfly.

To bead a lower wing, begin at a dot marked on the pattern. Slip the needle through a tulip bead, a seed bead, back through the tulip bead, and through the wing at the same dot. Sew a tulip and seed bead at each dot in the same manner, bringing the thread between the fabric layers from dot to dot. Bead the second lower wing in the same manner, reversing the direction of the wing for the opposite side of the butterfly.

Place the two upper wings together, aligning the center edges. Whip-stitch the wings together. Whip-stitch the two lower wings together. Whip-stitch the lower wings to the upper wings.

For the beaded body, cut a 15" length of 24-gauge wire. Thread a seed bead and an oval crystal on the wire until they are 1" from the end. Bend the 1" wire end around the seed bead and insert it back through the oval bead to secure the beads at the tail end of the body. Pull the wire end taut and trim off any excess above the

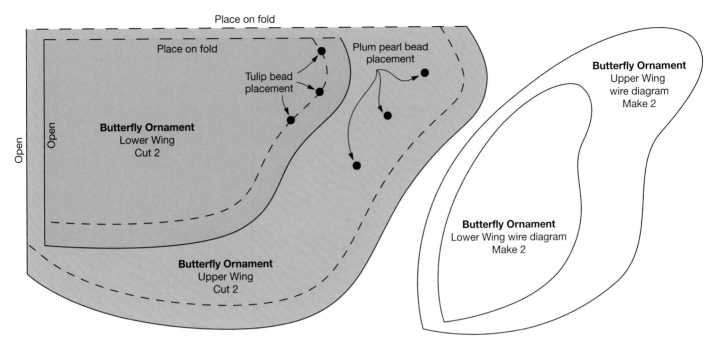

Place on fold

Place on fold

Tulip bead
placement

Plum pearl bead
placement

Butterfly Ornament
Lower Wing
Cut 2

Open

Open

Butterfly Ornament
Upper Wing
Cut 2

Butterfly Ornament
Upper Wing
wire diagram
Make 2

Butterfly Ornament
Lower Wing wire diagram
Make 2

crystal. Thread on a flower, crystal, pearl, crystal, and flower bead.

Position the beaded body over the center of the wings. Bring the wire from the top of the beaded body to the back of the butterfly as shown in the diagram *below*. Push the wire to the front between the upper and lower wings on one side of the body. Return the wire to the back between the upper and lower wings on the opposite side of the body, securing the center of the beaded body to the wings as shown *below*. Bring the wire to the head-end of the beaded body, wrapping it around the wire that runs along the back.

For the antennae, form a 4" loop with the wire and wrap the end around the bottom of the loop several times to secure. Trim off the excess wire. Cut the loop at the center, creating two antennae. For each antenna, thread six seed beads and five bugle beads on a wire, alternat-

ing the beads. Then thread on one tulip, one bugle, and one seed. Wrap the wire end three times around the tip of a needle-nose pliers. Trim off the excess wire. Repeat for the second antenna.

Cut a 7" length of 24-gauge wire and twist the center around the wire that runs along the back of the butterfly. Use the wire ends to attach the butterfly to a tree or wreath.♥

Dragonfly Ornament
Shown right.

YOU WILL NEED
⅛ yard of bright lavender cross-dyed velvet fabric
3½" square of gold/persimmon metallic cotton fabric
3" square of gold metallic cotton fabric
Polyester fiberfill
Matching sewing threads
24-gauge gold wire
Wire cutters
Needle-nose pliers
Beads: 10—6mm blue faceted rounds, 16—4mm blue or celadon faceted rounds, 8/0 periwinkle seeds, 11/0 purple metallic seeds, 8/0 celadon hex-cut seeds, and 11/0 silver triangle-cut seeds

INSTRUCTIONS
For the head, draw a 3" circle pattern; draw a 2¾" circle for the body pattern. Cut out the pattern pieces. Use the head pattern to cut one from the gold/persimmon metallic fabric. Use the body pattern to cut seven from the velvet fabric and one from the gold metallic fabric.

Thread a needle with matching sewing thread, bring the thread ends together, and knot. With the wrong side of a velvet circle facing up, fold ⅛" to the wrong side. Take small running stitches close to the folded edge, continuing to fold and stitch around the entire circle. Pull the thread slightly so the circle begins to cup with the wrong side of the fabric on the inside. Place a small amount of polyester fiberfill in the circle and pull the thread tightly so only a tiny opening remains at the center. Flatten the stuffed circle slightly to resemble a powder puff; knot the thread. Repeat for each of the velvet circles and the gold/persimmon circle. For the gold metallic fabric circle, fold and stuff in the same manner, but pinch the gathers outward for a pod look.

To assemble the body, cut a 25" length of gold wire. Form a 4"-long loop for the antennae at one end of the wire. Wrap the end around the bottom of the loop several times to secure. Push the opposite end of the wire through the center on the gathered side of the gold/persimmon circle and out the center of the flat side. Repeat for the seven velvet circles. Push the wire through the center of the gold circle from the flat side to the gathered side for the tail. Pull the wire tight, squeezing the stuffed circles together so the body measures 5" long. Wrap the wire three times around the pliers to secure the body. Do not cut the wire.

To bead the body, thread seven silver triangle-cut seeds, one 4mm faceted round, and seven silver triangle-cut seeds onto the wire end. Wrap the beading wire around the wire between the stuffed tail and the next velvet circle, drawing the beads around the side of the tail and into the center. Repeat for each velvet circle, adjusting the number of silver beads as needed to keep the faceted round bead centered on the side. Continue wrapping the beading wire around the wire between each velvet circle. Wrap the beading wire several times around the wire between the last velvet circle and the head. Trim off the excess wire.

Cut the 4" loop at the center, creating two antennae. For each antenna, thread on purple metallic seeds and celadon hex-cut seeds, alternating the beads, until the beaded area measures 1½". Wrap the wire end three times

around the tip of a needle-nose pliers. Trim off the excess wire. Repeat for the second antenna.

To create a beaded wing, cut a 48" length of gold wire. Wrap one end three times around the pliers for the top knot. Referring to Diagram 1 *below*, thread five 6mm blue faceted round beads onto the opposite end and slide them up toward the knot. Bend the wire into a 5"-long loop below the beads and wrap the wire several times around the top of the loop, leaving about 5" between the wrap and the top knot for the center axis of one wing. Extend the wire on the right side of the center axis. Do not cut the wire.

Beaded Wing Key:

- 10—6mm blue faceted rounds
- 8—4mm celadon faceted rounds
- 8/0 periwinkle seeds
- 11/0 purple metallic seeds
- 8/0 celadon hex-cut seeds
- 11/0 silver triangle-cut seeds

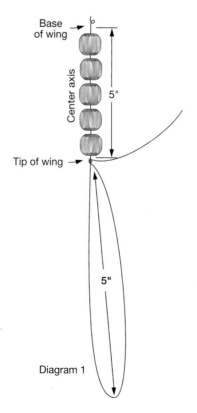

Diagram 1

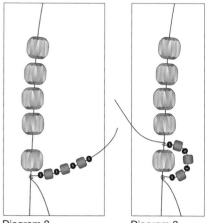

Diagram 2   Diagram 3

Alternating the seed beads, slide four purple metallic and three periwinkle onto the wire as shown in Diagram 2 *above*. Bend the beaded wire around the bottom 6mm bead to encircle the right side of the bead as shown in Diagram 3 *above*. Take the wire over the top of the center axis and wrap it once around the wire to extend on the left side. Repeat the beading pattern and encircle the left side of the second 6mm bead in the same manner. Continue the beading pattern to encircle alternating sides of the remaining 6mm beads.

Continue beading the wing, referring in order to Diagrams 4–9 *opposite*, and using the Beaded Wing Key *left*, for the correct bead placement and number and kinds of beads.

To finish the tip of the wing, cut the 5"-long loop, making two wire ends as shown in Diagram 10 *opposite*. Trim one end 1" shorter than the other. Working with the longer wire, slide on five silver triangle-cut seeds, one periwinkle seed, and five silver triangle-cut seeds. Bend the beaded wire into a small loop at the center bottom of the wing. Wrap the wire around the top of the loop so the two wires extend in opposite directions from the center axis as shown in Diagram 11 *opposite*.

Slide two silver triangle-cut seeds, one 4mm faceted round, two silver triangle-cut seeds, one 4mm faceted round, and 13 silver triangle-cut seeds onto the right wire. Bead the beaded

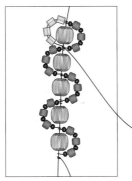

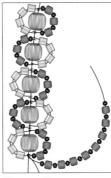

Diagram 4

Diagram 5

Diagram 6

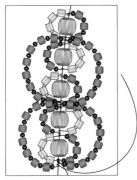

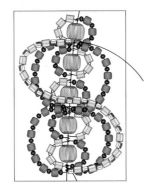

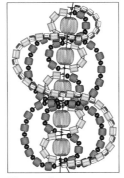

Diagram 7

Diagram 8

Diagram 9

Tip of wing

Cut

1"

Diagram 10

Diagram 11

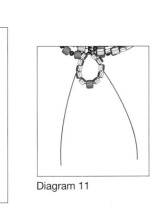

Diagram 12

2"-diameter Styrofoam ball
Spanish moss
16" of narrow cording

INSTRUCTIONS

Apply a light coat of pale gold metallic paint on the seashell. Immediately pour clear glitter over the wet paint, tap off the excess glitter, and set the shell aside to dry.

Cut the leaf spray apart. To make longer stems, cut two 4" lengths of florist's wire. Position a wire length on two leaves. Wrap the new stems with florist's tape. Wire together the three leaves with the leaves at different heights.

Use the paintbrush to apply a light coat of tacky glue to the pansies. Immediately pour the glitter over the wet glue, tap off the excess glitter, and set the pansies aside to dry. Trim the pansy bouquet stems short and wrap them together with florist's wire.

Cut the Styrofoam ball in half and trim it to fit snugly inside the shell; glue in place. Use the stems of the pansy bouquet to make a hole in the ball. Adjust the height of the bouquet if necessary and glue the stems in the hole. Glue the leaf spray behind the pansies in the same manner. Glue a layer of Spanish moss over the ball.

For the hanging loop, fold the cording in half and knot the ends together. Slip the cording around the base of the bouquet.♥

wire into a curve and wrap the wire three times around the center axis between the second and third 6mm bead from the bottom as shown in Diagram 12 *above.* Trim the excess wire and flatten the end. Repeat with the remaining wire on the left side.

Make a second beaded wing. To attach the wings, wrap the wires at the base of each wing around the wire between the head and the first velvet body circle. Use the excess wire to attach the dragonfly to a tree or wreath.♥

Pansy Bouquet and Sea Shell Ornament
Shown right.

YOU WILL NEED
Murex seashell
Pale gold acrylic metallic paint
1"-wide foam brush
Clear glitter
Velvet leaf spray with 3 leaves
32-gauge cotton-wrapped florist's wire
Florist's tape
Tacky glue
Paintbrush
Velvet pansy bouquet with about 5 pansies

Frosty Friends

This oh-snow-cool room wears the frostiest—and warmest—faces!
From the tree to the mantel to the walls, smiling snowmen and
snowwomen smile from tree trims, His and Hers felt stockings,
a floor sculpture, and wreath decorations. Enticed by an array of
techniques, you're sure to find a new project to try. Instructions begin
on *page 110.*

With a ready grin and cheery wave, this little snow pal, *left*, packs loads of holiday punch. The frosty design is created on a ready-made glass ornament using paint pens made especially for glass. Notice that the pen-painting is done on both sides; on a flat surface this technique adds dimension.

Once the tree is blanketed in wintry fun, take your snow-building enthusiasm to the floor. Pull out bags of fluffy fiberfill or batting to skirt the tree and the foreground in "snow." Then raise this frosty, 3-foot snow fellow, *opposite*. Packed with kid appeal, he's an easy stitch-and-stuff showpiece. The front, back, and bottom are cut from plain muslin and finished with a coat or two of acrylic paint to add sturdiness. Finish with twigs for arms, a wool flannel cap, and a wrapped scarf at the neck. Poised beside the tree, he'll play host to wrapped packages and guests all season long.

Get ready for some winter fun. This snow-packed cutie performs a trio of daredevil feats from the holiday tree. He can glide on wire skates, *above*, or ride on a tongue-depressor sled, *opposite*. He even slips on skis (but you'll have to turn to the instructions on *page 120* to see this one). The ornament's structure, consisting of a plastic-foam ball, wooden cups, and wooden beads, gets wired and covered with a fluffy snow-texture medium.

Rug hooking works country texture into this pretty snow face, *opposite left*. It's a miniature version of the tree's topper shown on *page 104*.

The snowflake juggler, *opposite right*, is embroidered in cool-blue outline, straight, cross, and French knot stitches. Softly padded, it's edged in gold trim and backed with red felt.

Hooked Snowmen

Shown on pages 104 and 109.

YOU WILL NEED

For both projects:
Tracing paper
Nylon netting
Fine-tip permanent marking pen
Rug-hooking burlap or monk's cloth
Rug-hooking frame or embroidery hoop
Rotary cutter, rotary-cutting mat, and a
    clear acrylic ruler (optional)
Rug hook

For each ornament:
Solid color wool: white, orange, rose,
    and black
Scrap of red plaid wool
6" length of cording
6" square of white felt
Fabric glue
Pinking shears

For the tree topper:
Solid color wool: white, dark gray, orange,
    rose, and black
Cream-and-black plaid wool
18×21" piece of white wool for the back
Polyester fiberfill
2 yards of 1½"-wide white ribbon
1½ yards of red plaid wool

INSTRUCTIONS

Prepare the Fabric

Machine-wash the wool pieces in hot water, and dry at high temperature in the dryer. Cut the wool into ¼"-wide strips, cutting carefully along the weave of the wool.

Trace the ornament pattern *below* onto tracing paper or enlarge the tree topper pattern, *opposite*, onto graph paper. Center the netting over the tracing paper pattern; trace the design onto the netting with a permanent marking pen. To transfer the design onto the burlap or monk's cloth, center the netting on the foundation and retrace the design using the marking pen.

To prevent fraying, tape or zigzag-stitch the edges of the foundation fabric and machine-sew along the outline of your design. Stretch the fabric tautly in a rug-hooking frame or embroidery hoop.

Hook the Design

For instructions on rug hooking, see *page 157.*

Ornament. Hook two rows of white to outline the face, following the outside curved shape of the design. Use orange to outline and then fill the nose. With rose, outline and then fill the cheeks. Hook the eyes and mouth black. Completely fill in the remaining open area of the ornament with white, following the direction of the previously hooked rows. Trim off the tops of the orange loops to sculpture the nose.

Tree Topper. Hook two rows of white to outline the face, following the outside shape of the design. Hook two rows of dark gray to outline the hat. Use orange to outline and then fill the nose. With rose, outline and then fill the cheeks. Hook the eyes and mouth black. Completely fill in the face with white, following the direction of the previously hooked rows. Fill in the hat with dark gray. Use cream-and-black plaid to hook the hatband.

Assemble the Pieces

Remove the finished design from the frame or hoop; trim the tails even with the looped surface. Place the hooked side down, on an ironing board, and cover it with a damp pressing cloth. Use a hot iron to press *Continued on page 112*

Hooked Snowman
Ornament

Continued on page 112

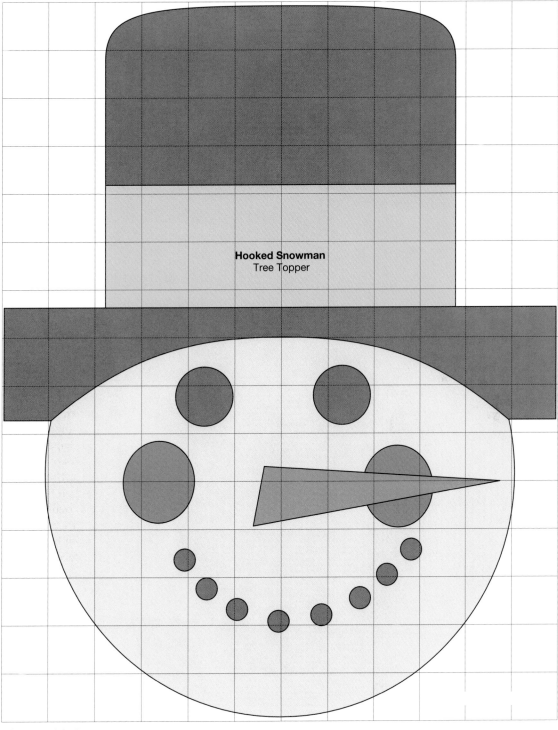

Hooked Snowman
Tree Topper

1 Square = 1 Inch

the entire back of the hooked piece. Remove the pressing cloth and let the piece lay flat until it's completely dry.

Ornament. Trim the foundation fabric just beyond the machine sewing line around the design. Fold the 6" length of cording in half and glue the ends to the top center back of the hooked piece. Glue the hooked piece centered on the white felt. When the glue is dry, use the pinking shears to trim the felt ¼" beyond the edges of the hooked piece. Tie a 1×10" strip of red plaid wool into a bow. Glue the bow to the top of the head.

Tree Topper. Trim the foundation fabric 1½" beyond the hooked edge of the design. Using the trimmed snowman as a pattern, cut a matching piece from the 18×21" piece of white wool for the back. With right sides together, sew the hooked front to the back along the hooked edge of the design, leaving a 4" opening at the bottom for stuffing. Turn the snowman right side out. Lightly stuff the snowman with polyester fiberfill. Slip-stitch the opening closed.

For the scarf, cut enough 13"-wide strips from the red plaid fabric to total 145" in length. Sew the short ends of the strips together to make one long strip. With right sides together, fold the strip in half lengthwise and sew the long edges together, using a ½" seam allowance and creating a long tube. Turn the tube right side out. To fringe the scarf, remove 1" of crosswise threads from each end of the tube. Tie a bow in the scarf and tack the scarf to the bottom of the snowman.

Cut the 1½"-wide ribbon in half. Sew the center of one ribbon length 3" above the center bottom on the back of the snowman. Sew the center of the second length 2" above the first ribbon. Tie the snowman to the treetop with the ribbons.♥

Designed by Donna Lovelady

Standing Snowman
Shown above.

YOU WILL NEED
Graph paper
1¼ yards of 45"-wide heavy white cotton duck fabric
18" square of red wool plaid fabric
White sewing thread
2 bags of polyester fiberfill
1 bag of plastic pellets

Delta Ceramcoat acrylic paints: 2 bottles of White 2505; 1 bottle each of Black 1506, Straw 2078, Opaque Red 2507, and Poppy Orange 2554
Delta Ceramcoat Gleams acrylic paint: Metallic Kim Gold 2602
Paintbrushes
2—24"-long branches

INSTRUCTIONS

Enlarge the snowman and base patterns, *opposite*, on graph paper. Cut out the pattern pieces. Sew all pieces with right sides together, using ½" seam allowances unless otherwise noted in the directions.

From the white cotton duck fabric, cut a snowman front and back, one base, and one 6¾×44" strip for the scarf. Using a pencil, lightly transfer the facial features and star buttons to the snowman front.

Sew the snowman front to the back, leaving the bottom edge open and two 1" openings for the arms as indicated by the dots on the pattern. Sew the base to the bottom of the snowman, leaving a 5" opening at the center back for stuffing. Trim the seam allowances, and clip the curves. Turn the snowman right side out. First stuff the top of the snowman with two bags of polyester fiberfill; then pour the bag of pellets into the bottom of the snowman. Slip-stitch the opening closed.

Apply a thick coat of White paint to all surfaces of the snowman and one side of the scarf. Let the paint dry. Beginning 2" from the end, paint ¾"-wide Opaque Red stripes across the scarf, spacing the stripes about 1" apart. Referring to the pattern and the photograph at *left*, paint the facial features and star buttons on the snowman. Paint the nose Poppy Orange and the star buttons Straw. Add touches of Metallic Kim Gold to the stars. Use black to paint the eyes, mouth, and eyebrows, and to outline the nose and star buttons.

For the arms, insert the branches into the openings on the sides of the body. For the kerchief, fold over 1½" on one edge of the red plaid fabric square. Wrap the folded edge around the snowman's head; knot or pin the corners at the center back of the head. To fringe the painted scarf, make 2"-long cuts spaced ¾" apart along the short ends of the scarf. Tie the scarf around the snowman's neck.♥

Designed by Heidi Boyd

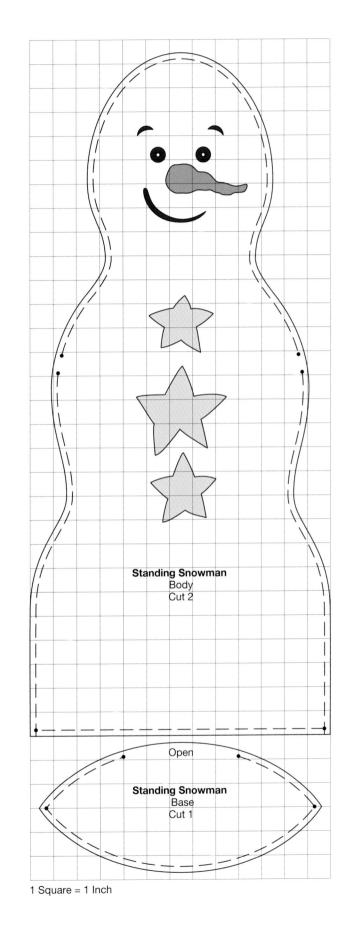

Standing Snowman
Body
Cut 2

Open

Standing Snowman
Base
Cut 1

1 Square = 1 Inch

Snow People Stockings
Shown above and on page 105.

YOU WILL NEED
For each stocking:

Graph paper

Felt: ⅓ yard of off-white, one 9×12" piece of orange, and two 9×12" pieces of light gold for the girl or one 9×12" piece each of green and red for the boy

¼ yard of plaid wool fabric

Buttons: 2—⅞"-diameter black for the eyes, 5—½"-diameter black for the mouth, 5—⅞"-diameter assorted buttons for stocking front, and 4 assorted buttons for boy's stocking cap

Matching sewing threads

#8 pearl cotton: black, orange, blue, green, and light gold

Polyester fiberfill

Powder blush

1 yard of 1"-wide wire-edged ribbon

INSTRUCTIONS
Enlarge the stocking pattern pieces, *opposite,* on graph paper. Cut out each pattern piece.

Cut the Felt
From the off-white felt, cut two stockings, two heads, and one 1½×7" strip for the hanging loop. From the plaid fabric, cut one heel, one toe, and enough 2"-wide strips to total 48" in length for the scarf. From the orange felt, cut one nose. For the girl, cut two hat crowns and two brims from the gold felt. For the boy, cut two cap crowns from dark green felt, and two cuffs from the red felt.

Sew the Stocking
Position the heel and toe on the stocking front; baste in place along the outer edges of the stocking, using a ½" seam allowance. Use one strand of pearl cotton to make random cross-stitches and straight stitches along the remaining edge of the heel and toe. With right sides facing, sew the stocking front to the stocking back, leaving the top edge open. Clip the curves; turn the stocking right side out. Referring to the pattern and photograph, *left,* sew five assorted buttons to the stocking front with pearl cotton.

For the hanging loop, fold the 1½×7" off-white felt strip in thirds lengthwise. Sew ⅛" from each long edge. Fold the strip in half to form a loop. Sew the loop ends to the top right corner of the stocking.

Apply powder blush to the cheeks on the head front for the face. Position the ⅞"-diameter black buttons on the face for the eyes and sew in place with black pearl cotton. Using two strands of black pearl cotton, straight-stitch the eyebrows and make long backstitches for the mouth. Add French knots to the ends of the mouth and sew five ½"-diameter black buttons over the mouth. Position the carrot nose on the face and sew in place with orange pearl cotton, making running stitches about ⅛" from the edges of the nose.

With right sides together, sew the head front to the head back, using a ¼" seam allowance and leaving a 3" opening at the top of the head for stuffing. Clip the seam allowances; turn the head right side out. Lightly stuff the head with polyester fiberfill; slip-stitch the opening closed.

For the girl's hat, pin the front hat crown to the back hat crown. Sew together the long curved edges of the hat, using a ¼" seam allowance. Turn the hat right side out. Position a brim on the wrong side of the hat front; sew, using a ¼" seam allowance. Repeat with the remaining brim and the hat back. Fold the brims up toward the right side of the hat. Use one strand of light gold pearl cotton to make running stitches about ¼" from the bottom edge of the hat. Make a bow with the 1"-wide ribbon; sew the bow to the hat underneath the front brim.

For the boy's stocking cap, pin the front cap crown to the back cap crown. Sew the long curved edges of the cap together, using a ¼" seam allowance. Turn the cap right side out. Position a cuff on the right side of the cap front and back. Use one strand of green pearl cotton to blanket-stitch the cuffs to the cap along the bottom edge and side edges. Sew four assorted buttons to the center top of the cap.

Place the hat or cap on the head and sew to the head. Position the head on the stocking front with the head extending about 4" above the top edge of the stocking. Use off-white pearl cotton to sew the head to the stocking at the front top edge of the stocking and underneath the chin. For the scarf, piece the strips as needed to make a 48"-long scarf. Sew the center of the scarf to the top center back of the stocking. Overlap the scarf ends or tie into a bow at the stocking front. Remove fabric threads to fringe the scarf.♥

Designed by Robin Kingsley

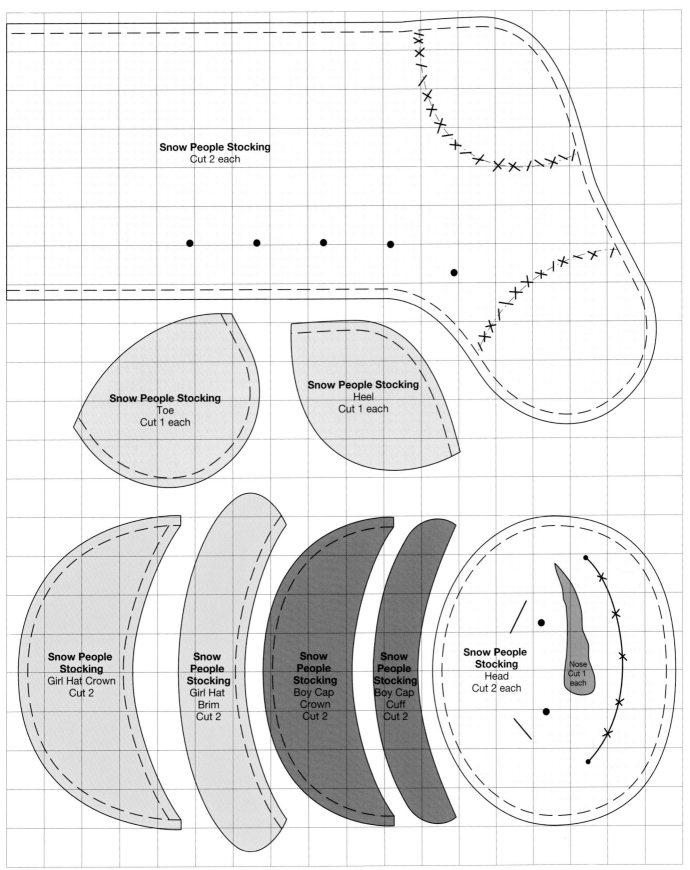

Snow People Stocking
Cut 2 each

Snow People Stocking
Toe
Cut 1 each

Snow People Stocking
Heel
Cut 1 each

Snow People Stocking
Girl Hat Crown
Cut 2

Snow People Stocking
Girl Hat Brim
Cut 2

Snow People Stocking
Boy Cap Crown
Cut 2

Snow People Stocking
Boy Cap Cuff
Cut 2

Snow People Stocking
Head
Cut 2 each

Nose
Cut 1
each

1 Square = 1 Inch

Felt Ornaments

Shown below and on page 105.

YOU WILL NEED

For each ornament:

Tracing paper

5×10" piece of Warm and Natural
   quilt batting

Felt: 2" square of orange and 1×2" piece
   of black

Scraps of wool, felt, or flannel

#8 pearl cotton: off-white and black

Orange sewing thread

Polyester fiberfill

Powder blush

4 black snaps

Jingle bell for stocking cap

9" length of fine cold cording

INSTRUCTIONS

Trace the patterns *opposite* onto tracing
paper. Cut out each pattern piece.

Cut the Fabric

From the quilt batting, cut two heads.
From the orange felt, cut one nose.
From the black felt, cut two 1" squares;
then trim off the corners of the squares,
creating irregular-shaped coal eyes.

From the fabric scraps, cut two
stocking caps, or two round hats, or
two earmuffs and one ³⁄₄×8" strip.

Sew the Ornament

Apply powder blush to the cheeks on
the head front for the face. Position
eyes on the face and sew in place with
one strand of off-white pearl cotton,
making running stitches about ⅛" from
the outer edge of the eyes. Using the
off-white pearl cotton, make a large ×
and then a + at the center of each eye.
Roll the orange nose triangle with long
edges together, forming a cone. Use
orange sewing thread to sew the long
edges together. Lightly stuff the nose
with polyester fiberfill and sew to the
face. Sew four snaps to the face for
the mouth with black pearl cotton.

Use off-white pearl cotton to blanket-
stitch the head front to the head back,
leaving a 2" opening for stuffing. Stuff
the head with fiberfill. Blanket-stitch
the opening closed.

For the stocking cap, pin the front
to the back with right sides together.
Machine-sew the long edges of the
cap together, using a ¼" seam
allowance and leaving the bottom

open. Turn the cap right side out.
Sew a jingle bell to the tip of the cap.
For the brim, fold up the bottom ¾"
of the cap. Place the cap on the
head and sew the cap to the head
underneath the brim. Fold the tip of
the cap down.

For the round hat, pin the front to
the back with wrong sides together.
Sew together the curved edge of the
hat with a running stitch about ⅛"
from the edge, leaving the bottom
open. For the brim, fold up the bottom
½" of the hat. Place the hat on the
head and sew the hat to the head
underneath the brim.

For the earmuffs, hand-sew gathering
stitches ⅛" from the edge of each
earmuff fabric circle. Pull the thread
ends to cup each circle; stuff with
fiberfill. Pull the threads ends to close
the openings and knot. Fold the ¾×8"
black fabric strip in half lengthwise;
sew the long edges together. Sew the
earmuffs and the ends of the fabric
strip to the front sides of the face,
curving the strip over the head.

For the hanging loop, use a needle
to thread the fine cording through the
top center of the ornament; knot the
ends of the cording together.♥

Designed by Robin Kingsley

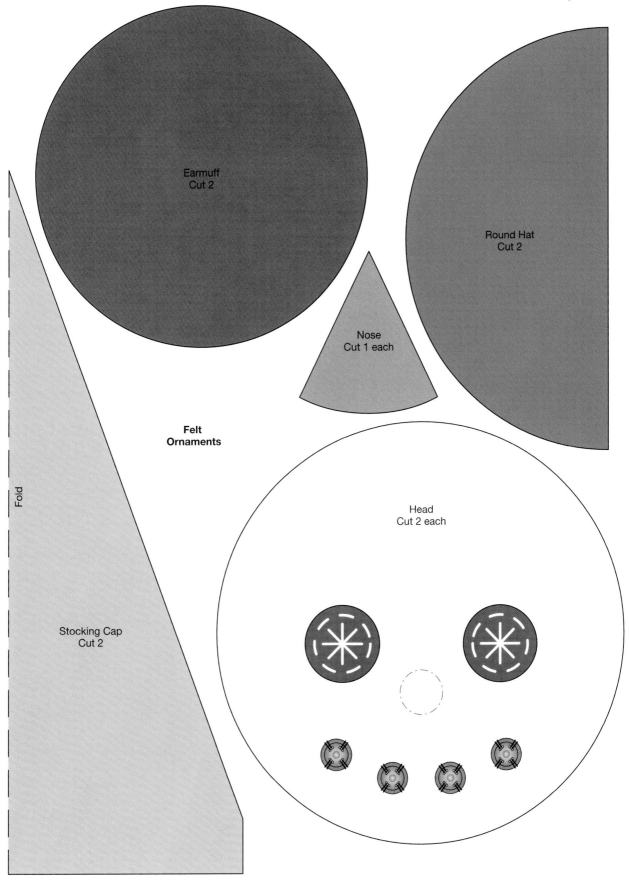

Earmuff
Cut 2

Round Hat
Cut 2

Nose
Cut 1 each

Fold

**Felt
Ornaments**

Stocking Cap
Cut 2

Head
Cut 2 each

Bluework Embroidery Snow People Ornaments

Shown on page 109.

YOU WILL NEED

For each ornament:
Tracing paper
9" square of 100% cotton
  unbleached muslin
Blue fine-tip Pigma pen
DMC blue (334) embroidery floss
Embroidery needle
4×5" piece each of medium-weight
  cardboard, fleece, and felt
13" length of ½"-wide gold trim
6" length of fine gold cording
Crafts glue

INSTRUCTIONS

Trace the desired pattern, *below* and *opposite*, onto tracing paper. Using a light source, center and trace the design onto the muslin square with the blue fine-tip Pigma pen.

Embroider the design using two strands of floss. Stem-stitch, and straight-stitch the outlines and straight lines. Satin-stitch solid areas. Make French knots for dots and running stitches for dashes. When stitching is complete, press from the back.

Trace the black oval pattern *below* onto tracing paper; cut out the paper pattern. Use the pattern to cut matching shapes from the cardboard and fleece. Glue the fleece centered on the cardboard. Center the embroidery on the fleece. Trim the excess fabric ½" beyond the edge of the board. Fold the edge of the fabric to the back and glue in place. Position and glue the trim around the edge of the ornament, overlapping the ends at the bottom center and trimming the excess. For the hanger, fold the cording in half to form a loop. Glue the cording ends to the top center of the ornament back.

Pin the oval pattern on the felt. Use pinking shears to cut out the oval ½" beyond the pattern. Center and glue the felt to the back of the ornament.♥

Designed by Robin Kingsley

118

Painted Snowman Ornament
Shown on page 107.

YOU WILL NEED
Tracing paper; tape
2⅝×4" 3mm glass oval shape with
    predrilled hole
DecoArt Liquid Rainbow paint:
    Raindrop and White Pearl
Fine-tip paint pens: black, blue, orange,
    and silver
12" length of ½"-wide silver ribbon

INSTRUCTIONS
Use warm, soapy water to wash the
glass oval, removing any fingerprints;
rinse and dry well. Trace the pattern,
above, onto tracing paper; cut out,
leaving a ⅛" margin around the design.
Position and tape the traced design to
one side of the glass oval.

On the other side of the glass, use
the black paint pen to draw the arms
and to make dots for the eyes, mouth,
and buttons. Use blue for the hat and
scarf. For the nose, make an oval dot
with the orange paint pen. Let the
paint dry for ten minutes.

Squeeze out small, medium, and
large circles of White Pearl paint for
the snowman's head and body. Use
Raindrop to fill in the open areas of

the scarf and hat. Let the Liquid Rainbow paint dry for 24 hours.

Turn the ornament over, and on the front side, randomly draw simple snowflakes and dots with the silver paint pen. Use the orange paint pen to draw a second carrot nose directly over the original nose. Let the paint dry.

For the hanging loop, thread the ribbon through the hole; knot the ends of the ribbon together.♥

Designed by Heidi Boyd

Sporty Snowmen Ornaments

Shown opposite and on pages 108–109.

YOU WILL NEED

For one snowman:

2"-diameter polystyrene ball for body
2—1¼" tall wooden candle cups for legs
Round wooden beads: 1—1¼"-diameter for the head, 2—⁵⁄₈"-diameter for upper arms, and 2—³⁄₈"-diameter for lower arms
Glue gun and hotmelt adhesive
Delta: Tub O' Snow and Fantasy Snow
Plastic knife
Black beads: 4 small for the mouth and 4 medium for the eyes and buttons
2 large white pearl beads
26-gauge orange wire
22-gauge green wire
20-gauge red wire
Wire cutters
Needle-nose pliers
Wide green crafts sticks:
3 for the sled; 2 for the skis
3 narrow red crafts sticks for the sled
13" length of 1½"-wide wire-edged plaid ribbon
12" length of ½"-wide red ribbon

INSTRUCTIONS

Refer to the photograph, *right,* to position the head and limbs on the polystyrene ball body for the different winter activities. Hot-glue a small bead to each medium bead for the arms. Hot-glue the head bead, the leg candle cups, and the assembled arm beads to the body.

Use a plastic knife to apply a thin layer of Tub O' Snow to the neck, and arm and leg connections and a ¼"-thick layer to the rest of the surfaces. To smooth out the surface slightly, spread Fantasy Snow over the face, stomach, and hands. Let the snow dry for 12 hours until it is slightly firm to the touch but still moist inside.

Use a toothpick to position the beads on the snowman. Firmly press two medium black beads into the front center of the body for the buttons. On the face, use two medium black beads for the eyes and four small black beads for the mouth.

For the nose, cut a 3" length of orange wire. Wrap the wire around the point of a pencil, creating a cone-shaped nose. Bend the wire end down from the nose. Remove the pencil and trim off the excess wire a scant ¼" below the base of the nose. Carefully press the nose onto the center of the face, pushing the wire end into the snowman's head.

For the earmuffs, cut a 3" length of green wire. Bend three loops into the center of the wire. Thread a pearl bead onto each end of the wire. Twist the wire ends to secure the beads. Shape the earmuffs over the snowman's head and press the beads into either side of the head. Temporarily remove the beads and then attach them with hot-glue.

To make skates, cut two 5" lengths of red wire. Shape each wire into a 1½" long skate. For the front of the skate, grasp one end of the wire with the needle-nose pliers and curl 2" of wire into a spiral. For the back of the skate, fold over 1¼" to the center of the wire, and then bend up ½" at a 90° angle to attach to the bottom of the leg. Hot-glue the wire end into the hole in the bottom of the leg.

To make skis, hot-glue a wide green crafts stick to the bottom of each leg.

To make the sled, line up three wide green crafts sticks side-by-side on your work surface with the center stick ½" in front of the others. Cut one red crafts stick in half. Hot-glue the halves across the sled about 1" from each end, connecting the wide sticks. For the runners, hot-glue the remaining two red crafts sticks to the bottom of the sled, centering them over the outside wide sticks. Position the snowman on the top of the sled; hot-glue in place. Cut a 5" length of red wire. Push a wire end through each hand. Hook the center of the wire around the center front of the

sled. Use needle-nose pliers to spiral the wire ends.

For the scarf, tie the 13" length of ribbon around the snowman's neck.

For the hanger, cut a 1½" length of green wire. Fold the wire in half, forming a loop; push the wire ends into the center top of the ornament. Thread the ribbon through the wire loop and knot the ends together.♥

Designed by Heidi Boyd

Snowman Icicle Ornaments
Shown at right.

YOU WILL NEED

For one ornament:
Waxed paper
Sculpey III polymer clay: Atomic Orange, Pearl White, and Red Hot Red
Black seed beads: 6 small and 2 large
Needle or toothpick
Crafts knife
Clear glass or plastic icicle ornament
Glass baking dish
Aluminum foil and baking parchment
Miniature glass marbles: silver and clear
Aleene's Platinum Bond 7800 Adhesive
Chenille stem
10" length of ¼"-wide sheer ribbon

INSTRUCTIONS

Cover your work area with a sheet of waxed paper. For one snowman, use one-fourth block of Pearl White clay. Knead the clay for the snowman between the palms of your hands until it is smooth and pliable. For the head, pinch off one-fourth of the clay and roll it into a squat ball, resembling a marshmallow. Set the head aside. Roll the remaining clay into a rounded ball. With your thumb and index finger, gently pinch two short legs at the bottom of the ball. Then pinch two even shorter arms at opposite sides of the ball. Smooth the head onto the top of the body, blending the clay together at the back of the body.

Use a needle or toothpick to position the beads on the snowman. Push two large black beads into the center of the body for the buttons. For the face, use two small black beads for the eyes and four beads for the mouth. Knead a tiny pinch of Atomic Orange clay and shape it into a carrot nose. Carefully press the nose onto the center of the face.

For the hat, use one-fourth block each of Red Hot Red and Pearl White clay; divide each color in half. This is enough clay to make several hats. Individually knead each piece of clay until soft. Use your fingertips to press each piece into a very thin slab. Stack the slabs, alternating the colors. Cut the layered slab in half and stack one over the other. Firmly press the layers together. Use the crafts knife to cut a triangular wedge from the clay for each hat that is about ½" wide at the base. Smooth the top and sides of the hat. Use your fingertip to make a concave opening in the bottom of the hat; press it on the snowman's head.

Pose the snowman at the top of the glass or plastic icicle ornament, gently pressing it to take the shape of the icicle. Make an icicle shape from aluminum foil, lay it in a baking dish, and cover it with a piece of baking parchment. Carefully pull the glass or plastic icicle away and lay the snowman over the parchment-covered aluminum-foil icicle. Put the baking dish in the oven and bake the snowman according to the instructions on the clay package.

When the snowman is cool to the touch, use the Platinum Bond 7800 Adhesive to glue the snowman to the icicle. To hold the snowman in place on the icicle, wrap a chenille stem around the snowman and the icicle until the glue sets.

Apply thin beads of glue to the snowman and down the length of the icicle. Immediately pour the tiny silver and clear marbles onto the wet glue. Let the glue dry completely.

For the hanger, thread the ribbon through the top of the ornament; knot the ribbon ends together to form a loop.♥

Designed by Heidi Boyd

Artichoke-Feta Cheesecake

Tarragon-Chicken Crepe Bundles

'Tis the Seasoning

M Christmas may surround us with glamour and glitz, but our fondest memories come from the heartwarming aromas and flavors of favorite holiday party foods. And nowhere are those scents and tastes more appealing than on a buffet table of well-seasoned appetizers. Just think about the sweet aroma of ginger as it's baking and the pine-fresh flavor of oregano sprinkled on melted cheese. These exciting spices and herbs remind us of holidays past and hint of faraway places. That's especially true at party time, when guests want little bites with big flavor. You'll whet their appetites for seductive herbs, spritely spices, and blends of both in this delicious collection of holiday appetizers, all perfect for party nibbling.

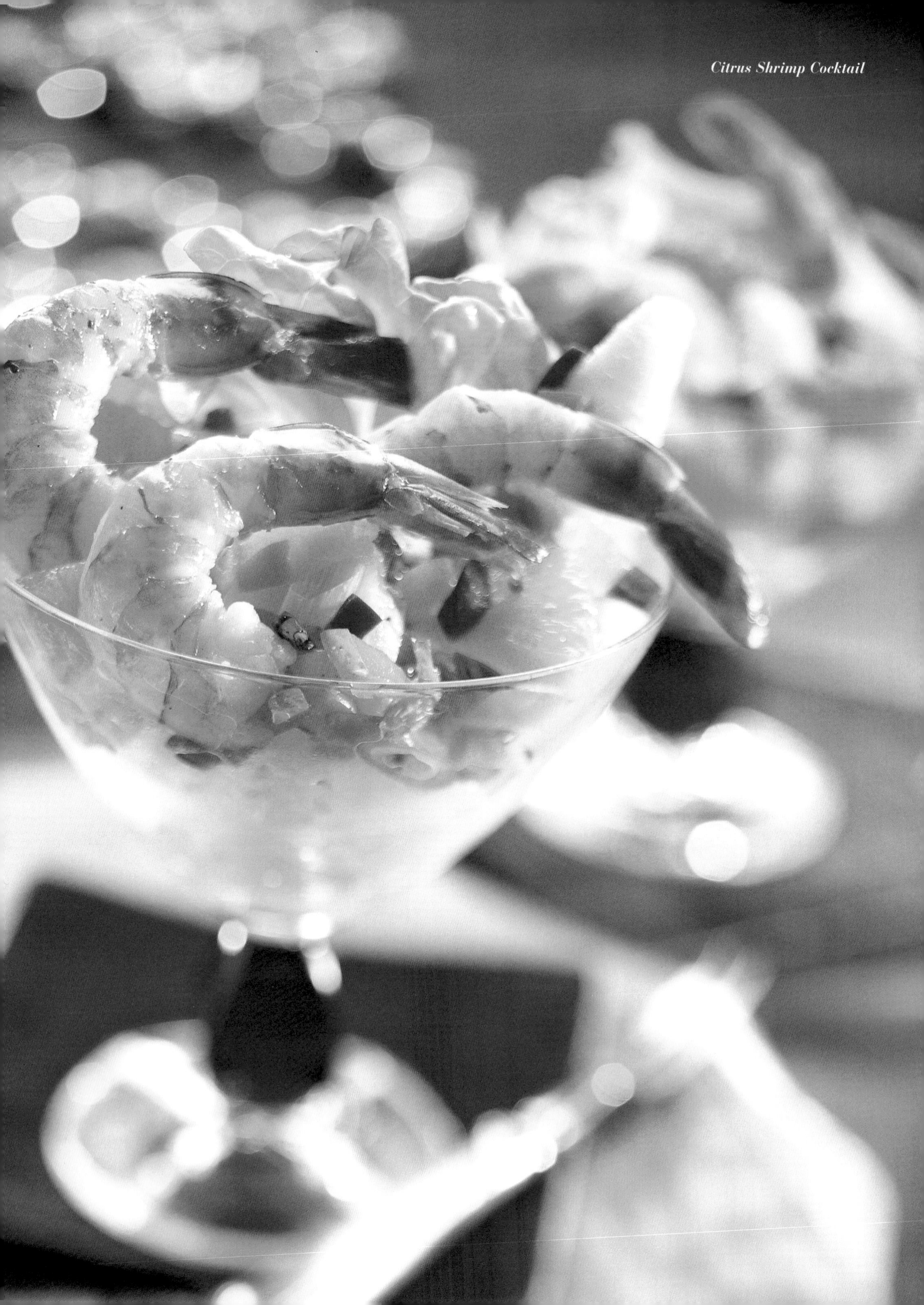

Citrus Shrimp Cocktail

Basil-Tomato Bruschetta

Greek Lamb and Cheese Strudel

Spicy Burrito Bites

Citrus Shrimp Cocktail. Anise seed stars and cinnamon plays backup in this colorful rendition of the classic seafood cocktail. Juicy grapefruit, orange, and pineapple really make the spices sing.

Basil-Tomato Bruschetta. A surprising hint of mint brightens the tried-and-true baguette topper— the beloved Italian combination of basil, tomatoes, and cheese.

Greek Lamb and Cheese Strudel. A dusting of nutmeg laces both filling and crust of this warm slice-and-eat phyllo pastry.

Spicy Burrito Bites. ¡Arriba! Cumin dances boldly forward, giving these hot 'n spicy tortilla wraps a singularly Mexican flavor.

Miniature Crab Cakes

Curry Pita Chips

Curry Pita Chips. Curry favor by brushing pita bread with curry powder—a seasoning blend of as many as 20 different spices and herbs. For a Mideastern or Indian-style appetizer, serve with hummus or yogurt for dipping.

Miniature Crab Cakes. Old Bay Seasoning is made for seafood. The mix is a mild blend of mustard, celery, salt, herbs, and spices that flavors these delicate crab cakes without overwhelming.

Jamaican Jerk Skewered Chicken. Okay, rub it in! At least that's how they do it in the islands with this spicy concoction of Caribbean spices, a medley of many flavors including allspice, ginger, and yes—red pepper. Don't worry, it's not too hot, especially when you serve it with mouthwatering tropical fruits!

Jamaican Jerk Skewered Chicken

Artichoke-Feta Cheesecake
To prepare fresh oregano for this appetizer cheesecake, put the rinsed herb in a custard cup and snip with kitchen shears. For a lower-fat version, substitute fat-free cream cheese for the regular cream cheese.

Tarragon-Chicken Crepe Bundles
For last-minute ease, you can make and freeze the crepes ahead of time, then just reheat and fill them before the party.

Artichoke-Feta Cheesecake

Prep: 30 minutes • Bake: 45 minutes
Cool: 45 minutes • Chill: 4 hours • Oven: 400°/325°F

¼	cup margarine or butter, melted
6	sheets frozen phyllo dough (about 18×14-inch rectangles), thawed
½	of a 6-ounce jar marinated artichoke hearts
3	8-ounce packages cream cheese, softened
1¼	cups crumbled feta cheese (5 ounces)
1	tablespoon snipped fresh oregano or 1 teaspoon dried oregano, crushed
¼	teaspoon garlic powder
3	eggs
¼	cup sliced green onions
	Fresh oregano (optional)

For crust, brush bottom and sides of an 8-inch springform pan with melted margarine. Unroll phyllo dough; cover with plastic wrap. Remove 1 sheet and place on a flat dry surface. Brush with margarine. Top with another sheet, staggering corners; brush with margarine. Repeat with remaining phyllo and margarine, staggering the corners all the way around. Lift into prepared pan, pushing phyllo gently around base. Allow edges to drape over pan. Make 2 slits in center to allow steam to escape.

Bake in a 400°F oven 8 to 10 minutes or until light brown. Cool on a wire rack. Reduce oven temperature to 325°F.

Meanwhile, for filling, drain and chop artichokes, reserving *2 tablespoons* of the marinade; set aside. In a large mixing bowl, beat cream cheese with an electric mixer on medium speed until smooth. Add feta cheese, snipped oregano, and garlic powder. Beat well. Add eggs all at once; beat on low speed just until combined. Do not overbeat. Stir in artichoke hearts, reserved marinade, and green onions.

Pour filling into crust-lined pan. Bake in a 325°F oven for 45 to 50 minutes or until center is still soft, but outside is firm when gently shaken. Cool in pan on a wire rack for 15 minutes. Loosen the crust for sides of pan and cool 30 minutes more. Remove the sides of the pan; cool cheesecake completely.

Cover and chill at least 4 hours or for up to 24 hours. Serve chilled or bring to room temperature. If desired, top with fresh oregano. To serve, cut into thin wedges. *Makes 14 appetizer servings.*

Tarragon-Chicken Crepe Bundles

Start to finish: 50 minutes

1	recipe Crepes (see recipe, right)
6	green onions
1	tablespoon olive oil or cooking oil
1½	cups chopped cooked chicken breast
¼	teaspoon ground white pepper
¼	teaspoon salt
½	cup reduced-sodium chicken broth
⅓	cup dry white wine
1	5.2-ounce package Boursin cheese
1½	teaspoons snipped fresh tarragon or ½ teaspoon dried tarragon, crushed
	Red sweet pepper strips (optional)

Make Crepes or thaw, if made ahead. For ribbons, clean green onions; trim and discard root ends. Thinly slice white parts; reserve 12 whole green top pieces. In a large skillet bring ½ cup water just to boiling. Add green onion tops; cook for 30 seconds. Immediately rinse with cold water; drain on paper towels and set aside.

In the same skillet, heat oil over medium-high heat. Add sliced onion, chicken, salt, and white pepper; cook just until chicken is heated through. Add broth and wine; bring to boiling. Reduce heat; simmer, uncovered, for 5 to 7 minutes or until the liquid is reduced by half.

Add cheese and tarragon; cook and stir until cheese is melted. Strain mixture, reserving liquid for sauce and solids for crepe filling. Cover sauce; keep warm.

Meanwhile, reheat crepes, if necessary. Spoon about 2 tablespoons chicken mixture onto each crepe; pull up sides to make a bundle. Tie bundle with a cooked green onion top. Serve bundles with sauce. If desired, garnish with red pepper strips. *Makes 12 bundles.*

Crepes: In a blender container, combine 1¼ cups *milk,* 1 cup *all-purpose flour,* 1 *egg,* 1 teaspoon *olive oil* or *cooking oil,* ¼ teaspoon *baking powder,* and ¼ teaspoon *salt;* cover and blend until smooth. Heat a lightly greased nonstick 7-inch skillet over medium-high heat. Remove from heat; spoon *2 tablespoons* of the batter into center of the skillet. Lift and tilt skillet to spread batter. Return to heat; cook for 1 minute or until light brown. Turn with a spatula; cook second side for 30 seconds. Carefully slide finished crepe onto a plate lined with paper towels. Repeat with remaining batter, keeping finished crepes covered. *Makes 12 crepes.*

Make-ahead directions: Stack crepes, placing 2 sheets of waxed paper between each crepe. Place in large plastic freezer bag; seal, label, and freeze for up to 1 month. To reheat, place stack of 6 crepes on a microwave-safe plate. Heat on high power for 60 seconds or until warm.

Citrus Shrimp Cocktail

Prep: 30 minutes • Marinate: 2 hours

1½	pounds fresh or frozen large shrimp in shells and/or sea scallops
1	teaspoon finely shredded red grapefruit peel
⅓	cup red grapefruit juice
¼	cup salad oil
2	tablespoons thinly sliced green onion
2	tablespoons chopped red, orange, or yellow sweet pepper
1	tablespoon white balsamic or wine vinegar
1	tablespoon honey
1½	teaspoons anise seed, crushed
½	teaspoon ground cinnamon
¼	teaspoon salt
	Butterhead lettuce leaves
½	medium pineapple, peeled, cored, sliced, and quartered
2	medium red grapefruit, peeled, thinly sliced, and quartered
2	medium oranges, peeled, thinly sliced, and quartered

Thaw shrimp and/or scallops, if frozen. Peel and devein shrimp, leaving tails intact. Cut any large scallops in half. Cook shrimp and scallops separately in lightly salted boiling water for 1 to 3 minutes or until shrimp turn pink and scallops are opaque, stirring occasionally. Rinse in a colander under cold running water; drain.

For marinade, in a large self-sealing plastic bag, combine grapefruit peel and juice, oil, green onion, chopped pepper, vinegar, honey, anise seed, cinnamon, and salt. Seal bag and mix well. Set bag in a large bowl; add shrimp and/or scallops. Seal and marinate in the refrigerator for 2 to 24 hours, turning the bag occasionally.

To serve, drain shrimp or scallops, reserving marinade mixture. If desired, spoon crushed ice into bottoms of 8 to 10 individual glasses or bowls. Line with lettuce. Arrange fruit and seafood atop. Drizzle with reserved marinade mixture. *Makes 8 to 10 appetizer servings.*

Basil-Tomato Bruschetta

Start to finish: 30 minutes • Oven: 375°F

2	tablespoons plus 1 teaspoon olive oil
1	clove garlic, minced
1	loaf baguette-style French bread, sliced into twenty ½-inch-thick slices
1	cup fresh basil
½	cup chopped green or yellow sweet pepper
2	medium tomatoes, seeded and chopped (about 2 cups)
1	tablespoon snipped fresh mint or 1 teaspoon dried mint, crushed
¼	teaspoon salt
¼	teaspoon ground black pepper
⅓	cup shredded ricotta salata or mozzarella cheese
	Fresh mint (optional)

In a small mixing bowl, stir together *2 tablespoons* of the oil and garlic; brush onto one side of bread slices. On a baking sheet, arrange slices, oil side up, in a single layer. Bake about 12 minutes or until toasted; set aside.

Citrus Shrimp Cocktail
You can serve this appetizer either in individual glasses or in a large bowl to let guests help themselves. A little crushed ice in the bottom keeps the seafood nicely chilled.

Basil-Tomato Bruschetta
You can toast the bread and stir up the topping ahead of time, then top the bread just before serving.

Greek Lamb and Cheese Strudel
Since the recipe makes two strudels, you can freeze one to serve at another party.

Spicy Burrito Bites
Keeping the tortillas warm until you're ready to fill them makes them easier to roll into burritos.

For topping, stack basil; roll up and slice crosswise into thin shreds. In a large skillet, heat remaining 1 teaspoon oil over medium-high heat. Add chopped pepper and cook about 2 minutes or until crisp-tender. Remove skillet from heat. Stir in basil, tomatoes, snipped mint, salt, and black pepper.

Spoon topping onto toasts; sprinkle with cheese. If desired, garnish with fresh mint. *Makes 20 appetizers.*

Greek Lamb and Cheese Strudel
Prep: 30 minutes • Bake: 15 minutes • Oven: 400°F

8	ounces lean ground lamb or ground beef
1/4	cup finely chopped onion
1/2	of a 10-ounce package frozen chopped spinach, thawed and well drained
1	5- to 6-ounce package soft goat cheese (chevre) or 5 ounces crumbled feta cheese (1 1/4 cups)
1	tablespoon milk
1	teaspoon finely shredded lemon peel
1/4	teaspoon salt
1/4	teaspoon ground nutmeg
6	sheets frozen phyllo dough (about 17×12-inch rectangles), thawed
1/4	cup margarine or butter, melted
	Ground nutmeg

For filling, in a medium skillet, cook lamb and onion over medium-high heat until no pink remains. Remove from heat. Drain off fat. Add spinach, cheese, milk, lemon peel, salt, and the 1/4 teaspoon nutmeg; stir until combined. Set aside.

Meanwhile, to layer phyllo, unroll phyllo dough; cover with plastic wrap. Remove a sheet of phyllo and place on a flat dry surface. Brush with melted margarine. Top with another sheet, matching edges and corners; brush with margarine. Repeat with remaining phyllo and margarine.

Using a sharp knife, cut stack of phyllo in half crosswise. Spread half of the filling lengthwise on each phyllo stack. (The filling should be within 3 inches of phyllo's long sides and 1 1/2 inches of short sides.) Fold short sides of phyllo over filling toward center. Fold a long side of phyllo over filling, then fold over several times.

Place phyllo rolls, seam sides down, on a large baking sheet. Brush with remaining melted margarine; sprinkle with additional nutmeg. Diagonally score the top of the phyllo rolls, making cuts 1 inch apart and 1/4 inch deep. (Do not cut completely through the phyllo.)

Bake in a 400°F oven for 15 to 18 minutes or until golden. Let stand for 15 minutes before serving. To serve, slice phyllo rolls along scored lines. *Makes 16 to 20 appetizer servings.*

Make-ahead directions: Make and shape phyllo rolls as directed, except do not bake. Wrap rolls in moisture- and vapor-proof wrap. Freeze up to 3 months. To bake, place frozen rolls, seam sides down, on a large cookie sheet and bake in a 400°F oven for 25 to 30 minutes or until golden. Slice along scored lines and serve.

Spicy Burrito Bites
Start to finish: 30 minutes • Oven: 350°F

1	to 2 fresh jalapeño peppers, seeded and chopped
1	teaspoon ground cumin
1	teaspoon olive oil or cooking oil
1	15-ounce can light red kidney beans, rinsed and drained
1/2	cup reduced-sodium chicken broth
8	7-inch flour tortillas
6	ounces reduced-fat cream cheese (Neufchâtel), softened
1	large cucumber, halved lengthwise and crosswise and seeded (2 cups)
1	small red sweet pepper, cut into thin strips (1/2 cup)
1/2	cup snipped fresh cilantro
	Salsa
	Cilantro sprigs (optional)
	Red chili pepper slices (optional)

In a large nonstick skillet, cook and stir jalapeño peppers and cumin in hot oil for 1 minute. Add beans; cook and stir for 4 minutes. Stir in broth; bring to boiling. Reduce heat; simmer, uncovered, for 10 minutes, stirring often. Set aside.

Spread *4 to 5 teaspoons* of the softened cream cheese onto each warm tortilla; spoon *2 tablespoons* of the bean mixture on top of the cream cheese layer, just below the center of each tortilla. Top with cucumber, sweet pepper, and snipped cilantro.

Fold in tortilla sides; roll up. Cut each burrito in half; serve with salsa. If desired, garnish with cilantro sprigs and chili pepper slices. *Makes 16 appetizers.*

Curry Pita Chips
Prep: 15 minutes • Bake: 8 minutes • Oven: 350°F

1/4	cup olive oil
1/2	teaspoon curry powder
1/4	teaspoon ground cumin
1/4	teaspoon ground red pepper
3	whole wheat or regular pita bread rounds

Stir together olive oil, curry powder, cumin, and red pepper. Split pita bread rounds in half horizontally. Brush both sides of each cut round with oil mixture. Stack rounds; cut stack into 8 wedges.

On a large baking sheet, arrange half of the wedges in a single layer. Bake in a 350°F oven for 8 to 10 minutes or until crisp. Repeat with remaining wedges. Store in an airtight container up to 1 week. *Makes 48 wedges.*

Miniature Crab Cakes
Start to finish: 45 minutes

2/3	cup fine dry bread crumbs
1/4	cup sliced green onion
1	teaspoon dry mustard
1	teaspoon Old Bay Seasoning
1/4	teaspoon pepper
1	beaten egg
1/3	cup mayonnaise or salad dressing
1	tablespoon Worcestershire sauce
1	pound cooked crabmeat
2	tablespoons butter or margarine
2	tablespoons cooking oil
	Snipped green onion (optional)

In a medium mixing bowl, combine bread crumbs, green onion, mustard, seasoning, and pepper. Add egg, mayonnaise, and Worcestershire sauce; mix well. Fold in crabmeat.

Using moistened hands, shape crab mixture into 1½-inch-thick patties. Place 1 tablespoon butter and 1 tablespoon oil in a large skillet; heat over medium heat. Add half of the patties and cook for 8 minutes or until golden, turning once.

Transfer crab cakes to an ovenproof serving platter. Keep warm in a 300°F oven while cooking remaining patties. Repeat with remaining patties, butter, and oil. Serve warm. If desired, sprinkle with snipped green onion. *Makes about 30 appetizers.*

Jamaican Jerk Skewered Chicken
Prep: 15 minutes • Marinate: 2 hours
Broil: 10 minutes

1/3	cup teriyaki sauce
3	tablespoons water
1/2	teaspoon Jamaican jerk seasoning
1	pound chicken breast tenderloins
10	5 to 6-inch wooden skewers

For marinade, in a small bowl, combine teriyaki sauce, water, and jerk seasoning. Rinse chicken; place in a plastic bag set in a shallow dish. Pour marinade over chicken. Seal bag; turn to coat chicken. Marinate in the refrigerator for 2 to 4 hours, turning bag occasionally.

Meanwhile, soak wooden skewers in water for 30 minutes.

Drain chicken, reserving marinade. Thread a piece of chicken onto each skewer. Brush with reserved marinade.

Arrange skewers on the unheated rack of a broiler pan. Broil 5 to 6 inches from heat about 10 minutes or until the chicken is tender and no longer pink, turning once. *Makes 10 appetizers.*

Curry Pita Chips
Serve these crispy pita wedges with purchased hummus (garbanzo bean dip) or plain yogurt. You can store the chips for up to a week in an airtight container.

Miniature Crab Cakes
If you prefer, you can bake the crab cakes. Just brush them with the melted butter (omit the oil) and bake in a 400°F oven for 15 to 18 minutes.

Jamaican Jerk Skewered Chicken
Temper these spicy sticks by serving them with juicy papaya, mango, and yellow or green kiwifruit. Yeah mon!

The Twelve Days of Christmas

"On the first day of Christmas my true love gave to me..." and so the ancient carol rings out as one lucky lady's true love expresses his devotion. For each of the twelve days that mark the Christmas observance, he's ready with a gift that's sure to attract her attention. Even the hardiest shoppers among us pale at the thought of trying to fulfill such a unique wish list. And every year, when a well-known department store tallies up the cost in present-day dollars, the astronomical sum makes us cringe even more.

While most people take this carol at face value—the story of a love-struck young man demonstrating his ardor through gifts—its origins are really more symbolic. According to letters written by Irish Jesuit priests, this song was actually a memory device to teach young Catholics the tenets of their religion during a time (1558 to 1829) when England forbade Catholics to practice their faith.

No matter what meaning really lies behind this centuries-old carol, the clever images and message of generosity have given the song a life of its own. On the following pages, the song turns to sweet fancy. Each of the twelve gifts is delightfully symbolized by a delicious dessert, from a glistening poached pear to a whimsical marzipan fruitcake drum. Ladies will dance and lords will leap when they sample this collection of dazzling treats.

A partridge in a pear tree is the first of the extraordinary gifts from the young man. And what could be easier and more humble than a golden pear to reveal one's heart? Crowned with licorice-flavored star anise, our *Poached Pears with Brandied Caramel Sauce* reflect love pure and simple.

Poached Pears with Brandied Caramel Sauce

1

Turtle Tart

On the fourth day of Christmas, *Calling Bird Meringue Cookies* beckon—billowing clouds of meringue as light as feathers. And on the fifth day, five golden rings appear—*Almond Spritz Rings*—dusted with silver and gilded with gold.

On the second day of Christmas, two turtle doves fly in. Our gift is a decadent rendition of turtle candies. *Turtle Tart* tempts with seductive truffle-like chocolate, a velvety stream of caramel sauce, and lightly toasted pecans.

On the third day of Christmas, say *bonjour* to three French hens. For alas, without eggs, we could not make the silky *Ginger Crème Brûlée*. *Mais oui!* This classic sugar-topped French dessert shows true *amour.*

Ginger Crème Brûlée

*Calling Bird Meringue Cookies
and Almond Spritz Rings*

Nutmeg Meringue Nests

Spiced Orange Mocha

Pumpkin-Pecan Cheesecake

Brandy Chocolate Cake

The Twelve Days of Christmas

On the sixth day of Christmas, it's time to feather *Nutmeg Meringue Nests,* not for six geese a-laying, but for a juicy filling of tropical fruit gems, sparkling with color and bursting with flavor.

On the seventh day of Christmas, start brewing the coffee so snow-white "swans" can swim creamily in steaming cups of *Spiced Orange Mocha.*

On the eighth day of Christmas, the eight maids a-milking must make sure there's enough cream cheese for moist and smooth *Pumpkin-Pecan Cheesecake.* It's udderly fantastic!

On the ninth day of Christmas, the lords will be a-leaping high, once they raise a gentleman's toast to intense *Brandy Chocolate Cake.* Cheers!

Orange Angel Food Cake

*Pecan Snaps with
Espresso Cream*

On the tenth day of Christmas, it's the ladies' turn to step out, dancing as lightly on their feet as our airy *Orange Angel Food Cake*. Serve it with a spoonful of *Apricot-Cranberry Compote.*

On the eleventh day of Christmas, pipers play their tune. Shape *Pecan Snaps* into lacy horns; then pipe in *Espresso Cream*. Hark the heralds!

On the twelfth day of Christmas, get ready for the big drum roll—twelve drummers marching up the walk, with your true love in the lead. This fanciful marzipan-trimmed *Royal Fruit Cake* makes enough for every drummer to have a slice or two. You won't miss a beat!

Royal Fruit Cake

Poached Pears with Brandied Caramel Sauce

If you want to top each pear with star anise as shown, save the two from the poaching liquid and use four additional star anise. Or garnish some pears with the cinnamon sticks from the liquid.

Turtle Tart

For the golden topping, make Brandied Caramel Sauce or heat a little caramel ice cream topping in the microwave oven for a few seconds.

Poached Pears with Brandied Caramel Sauce

Prep: 30 minutes • Chill: 8 hours • Cook: 30 minutes

6	medium firm Bosc or other pears
1	medium orange
6	cups water
1½	cups sugar
6	inches stick cinnamon
6	whole cloves
2	star anise
1	recipe Brandied Caramel Sauce (see recipe, *below*) or caramel ice cream topping

Peel pears, leaving stems intact. Cut a thin slice from the bottom of each pear so pears stand up straight. Through the bottom of each pear, use a melon baller to remove the core. Set aside. Remove peel from orange; reserve peel. Squeeze juice from orange.

In a 4-quart saucepan or kettle, combine orange juice, orange peel, water, sugar, cinnamon, cloves, and anise. Bring to boiling; reduce heat. Cover and simmer for 5 minutes. Place pears in liquid. Return to boiling. Simmer, covered, about 20 minutes or until pears are just tender. Cover and chill pears in the liquid for 8 hours or overnight.

To serve, use a slotted spoon to transfer pears to dessert cups. Garnish with star anise or cinnamon, if desired. Discard poaching liquid. Drizzle pears with caramel sauce. *Makes 6 servings.*

Brandied Caramel Sauce: In a small saucepan, melt ¼ cup *butter* or *margarine*. Stir in 1 cup packed *brown sugar,* ½ cup *whipping cream,* and ¼ cup *light-colored corn syrup.* Bring mixture to boiling; reduce heat. Simmer, uncovered, for 5 minutes. Remove from heat; stir in 1 tablespoon *brandy* or ½ teaspoon *brandy extract.* Let stand for 15 minutes to cool slightly. *Makes about 1½ cups.*

Turtle Tart

Prep: 30 minutes • Chill: 3 hours • Bake: 15 minutes
Oven: 350°F

1¾	cups pecans
⅔	cup sugar
2	tablespoons butter or margarine, melted
1	cup whipping cream
8	ounces semisweet chocolate, coarsely chopped
1	recipe Brandied Caramel Sauce (see recipe, *below left*) or caramel ice cream topping
½	cup lightly toasted, coarsely chopped pecans

Preheat oven to 350°F. For crust, in a food processor bowl, combine the 1¾ cups pecans and sugar. Cover and process until pecans are very finely chopped. With motor running, add melted butter in a steady stream. Process until combined. (Or, in a blender container, blend pecans and sugar in batches. Or, chop pecans and combine with sugar. Transfer to a medium mixing bowl; stir in melted butter or margarine.)

Turn pecan mixture into a 9- or 10-inch tart pan with removable bottom or a 9- or 10-inch springform pan. Press pecan mixture evenly onto bottom and about ¾ inch up side of pan.

Bake in a 350°F oven for 15 to 20 minutes or until crust is light brown on edge. Cool in pan on a wire rack.

For filling, bring cream just to boiling, stirring occasionally. Pour over chocolate in a medium mixing bowl. Stir until chocolate is melted and mixture is combined. If necessary, beat smooth with a wire whisk. Pour into cooled crust. Cover and chill for 3 to 24 hours.

To serve, remove side of pan. Cut into wedges. Spoon sauce over each serving. Sprinkle with the ½ cup pecans. *Makes 12 to 16 servings.*

Ginger Crème Brûlée

Prep: 30 minutes • Bake: 35 minutes • Chill: 2 hours
Stand: 35 minutes • Oven: 325°F

1½	cups half-and-half or light cream
¼	cup sugar
1	2-inch piece fresh ginger, thinly sliced
4	egg yolks
½	teaspoon vanilla
4	teaspoons raw brown or regular sugar or 1 recipe Caramelized Sugar Topping (see recipe, *right*)

In a medium heavy saucepan, combine half-and-half or cream, the ¼ cup sugar, and ginger slices. Cook and stir over medium-low heat for 10 minutes (reduce heat as necessary to prevent boiling). Remove from heat. Cover and let stand for 15 minutes. Preheat oven to 325°F.

In a medium mixing bowl, whisk together egg yolks and vanilla just until combined. Strain warm cream mixture and discard ginger slices. Slowly whisk the cream mixture into egg yolk mixture.

Arrange four 5- or 6-ounce ramekins or custard cups in an 8×8×2-inch baking pan. Set pan on an oven rack. Pour the custard mixture evenly into ramekins or cups. Pour enough hot water into the baking pan around the ramekins or custard cups to reach halfway up the sides of the dishes.

Bake in a 325°F oven for 35 to 45 minutes or until custards are just set. Remove custards from water bath; cool on a wire rack. Cover and chill for at least 2 hours or up to 24 hours.

Before serving, remove custards from refrigerator; let stand at room temperature for 20 minutes. Sprinkle tops of custards with the remaining 4 teaspoons sugar. Using a small, hand-held torch, slowly and evenly melt the sugar. (Or if you don't have a torch, prepare the Caramelized Sugar Topping instead.) Serve immediately. *Makes 4 servings.*

Caramelized Sugar Topping: In an 8-inch heavy skillet, heat 2 tablespoons *sugar* over medium-high heat until it begins to melt, shaking occasionally to heat evenly. Do not stir. Once sugar begins to melt, reduce heat to low and cook about 5 minutes more or until all of the sugar is melted and golden, stirring as needed with a wooden spoon. Quickly drizzle caramelized sugar over custards. Let stand a few minutes to set.

Calling Bird Meringue Cookies

Stand: 30 minutes • Prep: 30 minutes • Bake: 1 hour
Oven: 300°F

2	egg whites
¼	teaspoon cream of tartar
1⅓	cups sifted powdered sugar
2	tablespoons semisweet chocolate pieces

In a medium mixing bowl, let egg whites stand at room temperature for 30 minutes. Line 3 large cookie sheets with foil; set aside. Preheat oven to 300°F.

In the bowl, beat egg whites and cream of tartar with an electric mixer until soft peaks form (tips curl). Add sugar, 1 tablespoon at a time, beating after each addition. Beat for 6 to 7 minutes on high speed until sugar is almost dissolved and stiff peaks form (tips stand straight). The mixture should be very thick and glossy.

Spoon egg white mixture into a large self-sealing plastic bag. Snip about ½ inch off a corner. Pipe 20 to 24 bird designs about 1½ to 2 inches long and 1½ inches apart onto the cookie sheet.

Place cookie sheets in 300°F oven. Turn off oven. Let cookies dry in oven with the door closed about 1 hour or until dry and crisp but still white.

Transfer cookies to a wire rack; let cool. Place in a covered container and store at room temperature for up to 1 week.

On serving day, melt chocolate; put into a small self-sealing plastic bag. Snip a tiny bit off one corner. Carefully pipe eyes onto birds. Place on a wire rack until chocolate is set. *Makes 20 to 24 cookies.*

Ginger Crème Brûlée
If you have a small kitchen torch, use it to caramelize sugar on this traditional creamy French custard. Otherwise, you can caramelize sugar in a skillet and pour it over the chilled custard. C'est bon!

Calling Bird Meringue Cookies
To make the bird shape, squeeze a little meringue for the head, then move the bag clockwise and down to form a question mark. Make the lower body by moving the tip to the right, then back to the left, almost to the end of the question mark, then a little to the right. Stop squeezing as you pull up, forming the wing tip.

Almond Spritz Rings
Edible glitter and luster dust help these cookies shine like gold. You can buy glitter and luster dust wherever cake-decorating supplies are sold.

Nutmeg Meringue Nests
Trace around a 3-inch-wide jar lid or container to make a circular pattern for making these feathery meringue "nests."

6

Almond Spritz Rings

Prep: 15 minutes • Bake: 8 minutes • Oven: 350°F

3/4	cup butter, softened
3/4	cup shortening
1	cup sugar
1/3	cup almond paste* (about 1/3 of an 8-ounce can), crumbled
4	egg whites
1	teaspoon vanilla
1/4	teaspoon salt
4	cups all-purpose flour
	Edible glitter or gold luster dust (optional)

Preheat oven to 350°F. In a large mixing bowl, beat butter and shortening with an electric mixer on medium to high speed for 30 seconds. Add sugar and almond paste; beat on low speed until combined, scraping sides of bowl. Add egg whites, vanilla, and salt; beat until fluffy. Beat in as much of the flour as you can with the mixer. Use a spoon to stir in any remaining flour.

Force unchilled dough through a cookie press with a ½-inch star tip into 5-inch strips on ungreased cookie sheets. (Or, roll into 5-inch strips with hands, using about 4 teaspoons dough for each ring.) Form into rings. If desired, sprinkle with edible glitter and/or brush with luster dust.

Bake cookies in a 350°F oven for 8 to 10 minutes or until edges are firm, but not brown. Transfer cookies to a wire rack; let cool. *Makes about 60 cookies.*

*Note: For best results, use an almond paste made without syrup or liquid glucose.

Nutmeg Meringue Nests

Stand: 30 minutes • Prep: 30 minutes
Bake: 75 minutes • Oven: 300°F

2	egg whites
1/4	teaspoon cream of tartar
2/3	cup sugar
1/8	teaspoon ground nutmeg
1/4	cup orange marmalade
1	tablespoon sweet white wine or orange juice
1½	cups cut-up assorted fruit such as papaya, green or yellow kiwifruit, mango, carambola (star fruit), or pomegranate seeds

In a medium mixing bowl, let egg whites stand at room temperature for 30 minutes. Cover a baking sheet with foil; draw eight 3-inch circles on foil. Set aside. Preheat oven to 300°F.

In the medium mixing bowl, beat egg whites and cream of tartar with an electric mixer on medium speed until soft peaks form (tips curl). Stir together sugar and nutmeg. Add sugar mixture to egg whites, 1 tablespoon at a time, beating after each addition. Beat for 6 to 7 minutes on high speed until sugar is almost dissolved and stiff peaks form (tips stand straight).

Using a pastry bag fitted with star tip, pipe the meringue mixture onto the circles, building up the sides to form nests. (Or use the back of a spoon to spread the meringue over the circles, building up the sides.)

Bake in a 300°F oven for 15 minutes. Turn off oven. Let nests dry in oven with the door closed about 1 hour or until dry and crisp but still white.

Transfer nests to a wire rack; let cool. Place in a covered container and store at room temperature for up to 1 week.

Before serving, in a small mixing bowl stir together marmalade and wine or juice. Fill each meringue nest with an assortment of fruit; drizzle with marmalade mixture. Serve immediately. *Makes 4 servings.*

Spiced Orange Mocha

Start to finish: 15 minutes

- ½ cup packed brown sugar
- 4 ounces semisweet chocolate, cut up
- 2 ounces unsweetened chocolate, cut up
- 1 tablespoon finely shredded orange peel
- ½ teaspoon ground cinnamon
- 4 cups hot brewed coffee
- 1 cup half-and-half or light cream, warmed
- 1 recipe Whipped Honey-Orange Topping (see recipe, *below*)
- Finely shredded orange peel (optional)

In a blender container, combine brown sugar, semisweet chocolate, unsweetened chocolate, the 1 tablespoon orange peel, and the cinnamon. Cover and blend until chocolate is finely chopped. Remove half of the chocolate mixture; set aside. Add *2 cups* of the hot coffee to blender container; cover and blend at medium speed until chocolate is melted. Add *½ cup* of the half-and-half or light cream; cover and blend until frothy. Pour into 4 coffee mugs or cups.

In the blender container combine reserved chocolate mixture and remaining coffee. Cover and blend at medium speed until chocolate is melted. Add remaining half-and-half or light cream; cover and blend until frothy. Pour into 4 more coffee mugs or cups. Top each serving with a spoonful of Whipped Honey-Orange Topping and, if desired, additional shredded orange peel. *Makes 8 servings.*

Whipped Honey-Orange Topping: In a chilled medium mixing bowl, combine ½ cup *whipping cream,* 1 tablespoon *honey,* and, if desired, 1 tablespoon *orange liqueur* or *orange juice.* Beat with chilled beaters of an electric mixer on medium speed until soft peaks form (tips curl).

Pumpkin-Pecan Cheesecake

Prep: 30 minutes • Bake: 40 minutes • Chill: 4 hours
Cool: 1¾ hours • Oven: 350°F

- ½ cup finely crushed graham crackers
- ½ cup finely crushed gingersnaps
- 2 tablespoons finely chopped pecans
- 1 tablespoon all-purpose flour
- 1 tablespoon powdered sugar
- ¼ cup butter or margarine, melted
- 2 8-ounce packages cream cheese, softened
- 1 cup granulated sugar
- 4 eggs
- 1 15-ounce can pumpkin
- ¼ cup milk
- ½ teaspoon ground cinnamon
- ¼ teaspoon ground ginger
- ¼ teaspoon ground nutmeg
- Toasted pecan halves (optional)

Preheat oven to 350°F. For crust, in a bowl, combine graham crackers, gingersnaps, the 2 tablespoons pecans, flour, and powdered sugar. Stir in butter. Turn into an 8-inch springform pan. Press evenly onto bottom and about ¾ inch up the side of pan; set aside.

In a large mixing bowl, beat cream cheese and granulated sugar with an electric mixer until fluffy. Add 3 eggs all at once, beating on low speed just until combined.

Place *1 cup* of cream cheese mixture in a medium mixing bowl. Add pumpkin, 1 egg, milk, cinnamon, ginger, and nutmeg. Beat on low speed just until combined. Pour pumpkin mixture into prepared springform pan. Top with cream cheese mixture. Using a knife, gently swirl through layers to marble.

Place springform pan in a shallow baking pan. Bake in a 350°F oven for 40 to 45 minutes or until center appears nearly set when shaken. Cool in springform pan on a wire rack for 15 minutes. Loosen crust from side of springform pan. Cool for 30 minutes more; remove side of pan. Cool for 1 hour. Cover and chill for at least 4 hours.

Before serving, garnish with toasted pecan halves, if desired. Cut into wedges. *Makes 12 to 16 servings.*

Make-ahead directions: Refrigerate, covered, for up to 1 week, or freeze up to 1 month. Thaw overnight in the refrigerator.

Spiced Orange Mocha
This recipe makes eight servings, which need to be blended in two batches. You can easily halve the recipe to serve four.

Pumpkin-Pecan Cheesecake
Creamy layered cheesecake is a luscious change from traditional pumpkin pie. Layer the pumpkin and cream cheese batters, then swirl them together with a knife.

Brandy Chocolate Cake
For this sweet indulgence,
choose a top-grade chocolate.
While the cake is baking and
cooling, prepare the frosting,
glaze, and chocolate leaves.

Brandy Chocolate Cake

Prep: 1 hour • Bake: 20 minutes • Chill: 20 minutes
Cool: 1 hour • Stand: 1 hour • Oven: 350°F

8	ounces bittersweet or semisweet chocolate, cut up
2	cups all-purpose flour
1	teaspoon baking soda
¼	teaspoon salt
1	cup sugar
2	eggs
1	cup cooking oil
⅓	cup brandy
¾	cup buttermilk
¼	cup brandy
1	recipe Chocolate Butter Frosting (see recipe, *right*)
1	recipe Chocolate Glaze (see recipe, *right*)
1	recipe Chocolate Leaves (see recipe, *right*) (optional)
	Fresh raspberries (optional)

In a small heavy saucepan, melt chocolate over low heat, stirring often. Cool. Preheat oven to 350°F. Grease and lightly flour three 9×1½-inch round baking pans; set aside. In a small mixing bowl, stir together flour, baking soda, and salt; set aside.

In a large mixing bowl combine sugar, eggs, oil, and the ⅓ cup brandy; beat with an electric mixer on low speed until combined. Beat on medium speed for 3 minutes. Beat in melted chocolate. Alternately add flour mixture and buttermilk to beaten mixture, beating on low speed after each addition just until combined.

Pour batter into prepared pans. Bake in a 350°F oven about 20 minutes or until a wooden toothpick inserted near centers comes out clean.

Cool in pans on wire racks for 10 minutes. Transfer cakes from pans to wire racks; cool thoroughly with bottoms up. Using a long-tined fork, poke holes in the bottoms of the cake layers. Sprinkle each layer with 4 teaspoons of the brandy.

To frost, reserve about ¼ cup of the Chocolate Butter Frosting; set aside. Place a cake layer on a serving platter. Spread with some of the remaining frosting. Repeat layers twice, spreading about ¾ cup frosting smoothly onto top of cake. Spread sides of cake with remaining frosting. Refrigerate cake about 20 minutes or until frosting is set.

Carefully spread Chocolate Glaze over top of the cake, allowing glaze to drip down the sides. Stir 1 teaspoon *water* into reserved Chocolate Butter Frosting. Pipe frosting onto top of cake in a decorative pattern. Pull the tip of a spatula or knife in diagonal lines 1 inch apart across the piped lines. If desired, decorate with Chocolate Leaves and fresh raspberries. Chill to store. Let stand at room temperature for 1 hour before serving. To serve, cut into thin wedges. *Makes 20 servings.*

Chocolate Butter Frosting: In a small mixing bowl, beat 1 cup softened *butter* with an electric mixer on medium speed until fluffy. Gradually add 3¾ cups sifted *powdered sugar* and 1 cup *unsweetened cocoa powder*, beating well. Slowly beat in ½ cup *milk*, 3 tablespoons *brandy* or *milk*, and 1½ teaspoons *vanilla*. Slowly beat in an additional 4 cups sifted *powdered sugar*. Beat in additional *milk* or *powdered sugar*, if needed, to achieve a frosting of spreading consistency. *Makes 5¾ cups frosting.*

Chocolate Glaze: In a small saucepan over low heat, melt 2 ounces *bittersweet* or *semi-sweet chocolate*, cut up, with 2 tablespoons *margarine* or *butter*, stirring frequently. Remove from heat; stir in ¾ cup sifted *powdered sugar* and 2 tablespoons *hot water*. Stir in additional *hot water*, if necessary, ½ teaspoon at a time, until smooth. Cool slightly (about 5 minutes). *Makes about ½ cup glaze.*

Chocolate Leaves: Melt 6 ounces *semisweet chocolate* or *white baking bar*; cool. Stir in 3 tablespoons *light-colored corn syrup* until combined. Turn mixture onto a large sheet of waxed paper. Let stand at room temperature about 6 hours or until dry.

Orange Angel Food Cake with Apricot-Cranberry Compote
Serve the spiced fruit compote warm or cool with the citrus-flavored cake.

Gently knead for 10 to 15 strokes or until smooth and pliable. To make a lighter colored chocolate, knead some white chocolate into dark chocolate. If too soft, chill in the refrigerator about 15 minutes or until easy to handle. Or, if desired, knead in enough powdered sugar to make stiffer. (Store unused chocolate in a sealed plastic bag at room temperature for 3 to 4 weeks. It will stiffen. Knead until pliable before using.)

To make leaves, shape a portion of chocolate mixture into a ball. Flatten slightly; place between 2 sheets of waxed paper dusted with powdered sugar. Roll to ⅛-inch thickness. Using small hors d'oeuvre or cookie cutters, cut into leaf shapes.

Carefully lift the cutouts from waxed paper and place atop and around cake. If desired, place smaller leaves on top of the larger leaves. Cover and store at room temperature up to 3 days before serving.

Orange Angel Food Cake with Apricot-Cranberry Compote

Stand: 30 minutes • Prep: 30 minutes • Bake: 40 minutes
Cool: 2 hours • Oven: 350°F

1½	cups egg whites (10 to 12 large)
1	teaspoon cream of tartar
1⅓	cups extra-fine granulated sugar
1	tablespoon finely shredded orange peel
1	cup sifted cake flour
1⅓	cups water
2	6- or 7-ounce packages dried apricots, halved
1	cup dried cranberries
⅔	cup orange juice
⅓	cup granulated sugar
2	inches stick cinnamon
½	teaspoon vanilla
¼	teaspoon almond extract

In an extra-large mixing bowl, let egg whites stand at room temperature for 30 minutes. Preheat oven to 350°F.

In the mixing bowl, beat egg whites and cream of tartar with an electric mixer on medium speed until soft peaks form (tips curl). Gradually add the 1⅓ cups extra-fine sugar, about 2 tablespoons at a time, beating until stiff peaks form (tips stand straight).

Sprinkle orange peel over beaten egg whites. Sift about one-fourth of the flour over beaten egg whites; fold in gently. Repeat, folding in the remaining flour by fourths. Pour batter into an ungreased 10-inch tube pan. Gently cut through batter to remove any large air pockets.

Bake on the lowest rack in a 350°F oven about 40 minutes or until top springs back when lightly touched. Immediately invert cake (leave in pan); cool thoroughly. Using a narrow metal spatula, loosen sides of cake from pan; remove cake. Place cake on a serving platter.

Meanwhile, for compote, in a medium saucepan combine the water, apricots, cranberries, orange juice, the ⅓ cup sugar, the cinnamon, vanilla, and almond extract. Bring to boiling; reduce heat. Simmer, covered, for 10 minutes. Remove from heat. Discard cinnamon. Keep warm or let cool.

To serve, slice the cake. Serve the compote warm or cool with cake. *Makes 12 servings.*

Pecan Snaps with Espresso Cream

Prep: 40 minutes • Bake: 7 minutes per batch
Oven: 350°F

¼	cup packed brown sugar
3	tablespoons butter, melted
2	tablespoons dark-colored corn syrup
1	tablespoon coffee liqueur or coffee
½	cup finely chopped pecans
¼	cup all-purpose flour
1	cup whipping cream
¼	cup sifted powdered sugar
4	teaspoons instant espresso coffee powder
	Grated chocolate (optional)

Preheat oven to 350°F. Line a cookie sheet with foil. Grease foil; set aside. In a small mixing bowl, stir together brown sugar, melted butter, corn syrup, and coffee liqueur or coffee. Stir in pecans and flour until combined.

Drop batter by level teaspoons 3 inches apart, or level tablespoons 5 inches apart, onto the prepared cookie sheet, fitting only 4 or 5 cookies at a time. Bake in a 350°F oven for 7 to 8 minutes for smaller cookies or 8 to 10 minutes for larger cookies or until cookies are bubbly and a deep golden brown.

Pecan Snaps with Espresso Cream
Bake the lacy rolled cookies in advance. Then just before serving, whip up the coffee-flavored cream and pipe it into the cookies.

11

Royal Fruit Cake
For best results on the marzipan coating, we suggest using an almond paste made without syrup or glucose.

12

Let stand on the cookie sheet for 1 to 2 minutes or until set. Quickly remove a cookie; roll cookie around a metal cone or the greased handle of a wooden spoon. When firm, slide the cookie off the cone; cool completely on a wire rack. Repeat with remaining cookies, one at a time. (If cookies harden before you can shape them, reheat in the oven about 1 minute or until softened.)

Up to 30 minutes before serving, in a large mixing bowl, beat whipping cream, powdered sugar, and coffee powder with an electric mixer on low speed until soft peaks form (tips curl). Pipe or spoon whipped cream into each cookie. If desired, sprinkle with grated chocolate. *Makes 30 cookies.*

Make-ahead directions: Bake, shape, and cool cookies as directed. Arrange in a single layer in a freezer container and freeze for up to 1 month. To serve, thaw cookies for 15 minutes. Prepare the whipped cream filling and fill the cookies as directed.

Royal Fruit Cake

Prep: 1½ hours • Bake: 1 hour • Cool: 2 hours
Chill: 1 week • Oven: 300°F

2	cups all-purpose flour
1	teaspoon ground cinnamon
½	teaspoon baking powder
¼	teaspoon baking soda
¼	teaspoon ground nutmeg
¼	teaspoon ground cloves
1½	cups currants
1½	cups dark or golden raisins
1½	cups diced mixed candied fruits and peels
1	cup candied red and/or green cherries
½	cup almonds, ground*
4	eggs
1	cup sugar
¾	cup butter, melted
½	cup rum, brandy, or orange juice
3	tablespoons lemon juice
	Rum, brandy, or orange juice (about ⅓ cup)
3	8-ounce cans almond paste
¾	cup canned vanilla frosting
3	to 4 tablespoons light-colored corn syrup
	Red, green, or yellow food coloring paste

Preheat oven to 300°F. Grease bottom and sides of two 9×1½-inch round baking pans. Line bottoms with waxed paper. Grease paper; sprinkle bottom and sides of pans lightly with flour; set aside.

In a very large mixing bowl, stir together flour, cinnamon, baking powder, baking soda, nutmeg, and cloves. Stir in currants, raisins, fruits and peels, cherries, and almonds. Set aside.

In a medium mixing bowl, beat eggs slightly with a fork. Add sugar, butter, ½ cup rum, and lemon juice; stir until combined. Stir egg mixture into fruit mixture; turn mixture into the prepared pans.

Bake in a 300°F oven for 1 to 1¼ hours or until a toothpick inserted near the centers comes out clean. (If necessary, cover pans loosely with foil after 1 hour to prevent overbrowning.) Cool in pans on wire racks for 20 minutes; loosen edges. Remove cakes from pans. Cool thoroughly on wire racks.

Wrap cake layers separately in 100-percent cotton cheesecloth moistened with additional rum, brandy, or juice. Wrap with plastic wrap or place in large self-sealing plastic bags. Store in the refrigerator for 1 to 2 weeks. Remoisten cheesecloth with a little additional rum, if it becomes dry.

To assemble, place ⅔ of a can of almond paste between 2 sheets of plastic wrap; press flat with hands. Roll out to just larger than a 9-inch circle (it should be slightly thinner than ⅛ inch). With a 9-inch round cake pan or cutout, use a pizza cutter to trace and cut a 9-inch circle, reserving trimmings. Repeat to create another circle. Cover circles with plastic wrap; set aside.

Roll out the contents of 1 can of almond paste between 2 sheets of plastic wrap into a 14×6-inch rectangle; cut into two 13×2½-inch rectangles.

Unwrap cake layers. Place 1 cake layer, top side down, on a serving plate. Top with 1 circle of almond paste. Spread with frosting. Top with remaining cake layer, top side down. Brush the top and sides of cake with corn syrup.

Wrap the two 13×2½-inch almond paste

Decorating the cake

To make the cake look like a drum as pictured *above*, you'll need to shape red, green, and yellow almond paste into decorations.

Roll out red almond paste to a 14×3-inch rectangle. Using a pizza cutter and a ruler, cut the red paste rectangle into four ½-inch-wide strips.

Roll out green paste to a 6×3-inch rectangle. Cut the green paste rectangle into about eighteen 3×¼-inch strips.

Roll out yellow paste to a ⅛-inch thickness. Using small hors d'oeuvre cutters, cut the yellow paste into stars or other desired shapes.

rectangles around cake to fit, brushing with corn syrup to hold edges together. Top with the other circle of almond paste. Cover cake with plastic wrap.

Divide remaining almond paste and trimmings in half. Color 1 half with red food coloring. Remove *2 tablespoons* plain almond paste; color with yellow food coloring. Color remaining almond paste with green food coloring. Put each color of almond paste between sheets of plastic wrap.

Roll out red almond paste to a 14×3-inch rectangle. Cut the red paste rectangle into four ½-inch-wide strips. Roll out green paste to a 6×3-inch rectangle. Cut the green paste rectangle into about eighteen 3×¼-inch strips. Roll out yellow paste to a ⅛-inch thickness. Using small hors d'oeuvre cutters, cut the yellow paste into stars or other

desired shapes. (See photograph, *above*).

Decorate the cake to look like a toy drum (see photograph, *above right*), brushing with corn syrup as necessary to help almond paste decorations stick to the cake. Arrange the green strips on alternating diagonal angles all around the cake. Wrap 2 long red strips each around the top and bottom of cake. Place the yellow stars between every other green strip. Cover the cake with plastic wrap until ready to serve. To serve, cut into wedges. *Makes 20 servings.*

*Note: Use a grinder, blender, or food processor to grind the almonds.

Gift Ideas

When you give something beautifully handmade to family and friends, it says "you're special to me" in a way no purchased gift can. Our gift collection offers heartfelt ideas for giving at Christmas and throughout the year. Instructions begin on *page 152*.

Wrap little—and big—hands in fleecy bundles of love and warmth. Mitten pairs stitched with elasticized wrists, *opposite,* are quick to make as stocking stuffers and for impromptu gift exchanges. Sew them in batches so you'll have the right size on hand. For a sweet impression, stitch rickrack into the seamline.

More than an extravagance of rich fabrics, embroidery, and cording, cushy neck rolls, *above,* make gifts of soothing comfort. Give one, or a pair, to ornament a chair or lend support for reading in bed.

This butterfly pincushion, *above,* proves something practical can also be beautiful. Like a crazy quilt, the felt is richly layered, sculpted, then lavishly embroidered. Other distinctive touches include a gathered and padded head, tufted body, and beaded chenille-stem antennae.

Personalize purchased bath slippers for everyone in the family, *opposite.* Simply monogram a felt appliqué for each slipper; then hand-sew the appliqués to the toes.

All designs were created by Mary Jo Hiney.

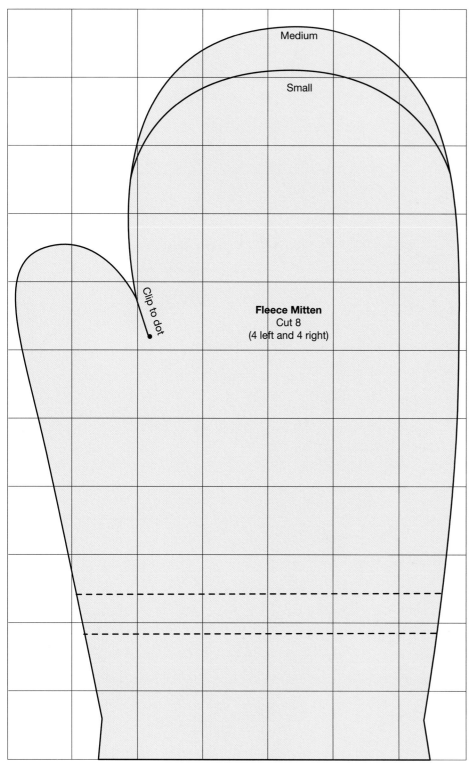

Medium

Small

Clip to dot

Fleece Mitten
Cut 8
(4 left and 4 right)

1 square = 1 inch

Fleece Mittens
Shown on page 148.

YOU WILL NEED
Graph paper
$\frac{1}{8}$ yard of polar fleece
$\frac{5}{8}$ yard of $\frac{5}{8}$"-wide ribbon
    for casing
$\frac{1}{2}$ yard of $\frac{1}{4}$"-wide elastic
1 yard of $\frac{1}{2}$"-wide rickrack (optional)

INSTRUCTIONS
Enlarge the desired mitten pattern, *left,* onto graph paper; cut it out. Use the pattern to cut eight mittens from the fleece. Sew all pieces with right sides together, using $\frac{1}{4}$" seam allowances unless otherwise noted.

To double-layer the mittens, layer together the mitten pieces in pairs for the fronts and backs; treat each pair as if one mitten piece. If desired, baste rickrack around the finger area on the right side of each mitten front. Sew the mitten fronts to the backs on the side opposite the thumb, beginning at the bottom edge and stopping as indicated on the pattern.

Open up the mitten and finger-press the seam allowances open. Cut the ribbon for the casing in half. Position a length of ribbon on the right side of both the front and the back of the mitten, about 2" above the bottom edges. Sew the ribbons in place along the long edges. Cut two 7" lengths of elastic. Insert a piece of elastic through each casing. Sew the elastic ends to the side edges of the mitten, adjusting the length as needed to fit comfortably around the wrist.

With right sides together, continue to sew the mitten fronts to the backs. Clip the seam to the dot as indicated on the pattern. Turn the mittens right side out. Evenly trim the bottom edges of the mittens if necessary. Turn under the bottom edges and finish with a decorative or elastic zigzag-stitch.♥

Beaded Bolster Pillow
Dove

Beaded Bolster Pillows
Shown above and on page 149.

YOU WILL NEED
For each pillow:
Tracing paper
$7/8$ yard of 44"-wide silk
   shimmer organza
$1/2$ yard of 44"-wide ivory broadcloth
Seed beads, Size 11/1: 1 package
   each of 2 or 3 colors to
   complement fabric
1 package of medium bugle
   beads to complement fabric
Navy blue gel pen
Beading needle
Matching sewing thread
Low-loft crib-size quilt batting or purchased
   bolster pillow form
$1^1/2$ yards of $1/4$"-diameter cording
   to match fabric
Fray Check liquid plastic
Tape

INSTRUCTIONS
Trace the desired patterns,
above and *right,* onto tracing paper.
   Press under 5" on each long raw
edge of the organza. Tape the traced
pattern onto a flat work surface.
Position and tape the organza, right
side up, over the tracing with the
design centered between the pressed
edges and the bottom of the pattern 3"
from one selvage edge of the fabric.

Beaded Bolster Pillow
Angel

153

Use the gel pen to trace the design lines onto the organza.

Thread the beading needle with matching sewing thread; knot the ends together. Starting at the beginning of a design line, bring the needle up from the back of the fabric, making two tiny stitches to secure the knot. Pick up one bugle and three seed beads with the needle and slide the beads down to the fabric. Following the design line, bring the needle to the back of the fabric at the end of the beads, and then back to the front between the bugle and the first seed bead. Bring the needle through the seed beads and pick up a bugle and three seed beads to repeat the pattern. Continue to cover the design lines by attaching beads in this pattern, randomly changing the seed bead colors. Adjust the bead pattern as needed to fit the design lines, using just seed beads for tight curves.

To make the pillow form, cut an 18" square from broadcloth; press under ½" on opposite edges. With right sides facing, fold the broadcloth in half, aligning the raw edges. Use a ½" seam allowance to sew the raw edges together, forming a tube; turn right side out. Hand-sew gathering stitches ¼" from each pressed edge. Slip the tube over the batting roll. Tightly pull the gathering threads to cover the ends of the roll with broadcloth; knot. If using a purchased pillow form, cover with broadcloth in the same manner.

Press the organza if necessary. Place the fabric, wrong side up, on your work surface. Center the pillow form on the unbeaded selvage edge of the organza; hand-sew the edge to the pillow form. Wrap the organza around the pillow form. Pin the remaining selvage edge to the pillow; use a needle and thread to tack the ends of the pillow form in place. Wrap a piece of tape around the center of the cording; cut in half through the tape. Tie a cording length into a bow around the fabric at each end of the pillow form. Apply Fray Check to the cording ends or tie a knot.♥

Monogrammed Slippers

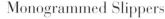

Shown below and on page 151.

YOU WILL NEED
Purchased slippers
White paper
2½"-diameter circle of template plastic or cardboard
Gel ink pen to match floss
3×6" piece of felt
Rayon embroidery floss
Embroidery needle
Pinking shears

INSTRUCTIONS
Trace the desired letters *opposite* onto white paper. Using a gel pen, trace the plastic circle onto the felt twice. Using the letters as a guide, practice writing the letters on scrap paper. When you are pleased with your drawn letters, center and draw a letter onto each felt circle. Use three plies of floss to outline-stitch over the drawn letters. Using pinking shears, cut out the circles just inside the drawn line. Tack each circle to the center front of each slipper using one ply of floss.♥

Butterfly Pincushion
Shown on page 150.

YOU WILL NEED
Tracing paper
National Nonwovens felt: 9×12" piece each of aquamarine, baby blue, cinnamon, copper, mustard, peacock, and teal
DMC rayon embroidery floss in six assorted colors
Sewing thread: cream and teal
6" length of aqua chenille stem
2—5mm rust beads
Chenille embroidery needle, Size 18 or 20
Polyester fiberfill

INSTRUCTIONS
Trace the patterns on *page 156* onto tracing paper; cut out the pieces.

From the teal felt, cut one butterfly for the back, one 2¼×3" rectangle for the scissors pocket, one center body, and one 2"-diameter circle for the head.

Monogrammed Slippers
Alphabet

Gift Ideas

From mustard felt, cut one body for the front. From copper felt, cut two upper wings. From baby blue felt, cut two bottom lower wings. From cinnamon felt, cut two top lower wings and two dots. From peacock felt, cut four petal designs. From aquamarine felt, cut two teardrop designs.

Refer to the photograph, *right,* and the pattern, *below,* to position the felt shapes on the front body and as a guide for embroidery. Pin or baste the shapes in place and stitch in the order that follows.

Position the lower wing shapes to the front body. Use cream sewing thread to whipstitch the top and center edges of the lower wing shapes to the body. Use two strands of floss to straight-stitch the remaining edges of the lower wing shapes in place, using a different color of floss for each shape.

Pin the upper wing shapes to the body. Use two strands of floss to straight-stitch the upper wings to the body. Use two strands of floss to attach the petal and teardrop designs with V-shaped straight stitches. On the dots, use two strands of floss to make eight straight stitches into the center of the circle.

Position the center body on the front body. Use teal sewing thread to whipstitch the center body to the body. Use three strands of floss to outline-stitch along the edges of the center body.

With right sides facing out, center and pin the pincushion front to the pincushion back. Use three strands of floss to blanket-stitch the pieces together, leaving a small opening for stuffing. Firmly stuff the pincushion with polyester fiberfill. Blanket-stitch the opening closed.

For the head, use teal sewing thread to hand-sew gathering stitches around the outer edge of the 2"-diameter teal felt circle. Pull the thread ends to cup the circle; stuff lightly with fiberfill. Pull the thread ends to close the opening and knot. Thread a needle with a 1¼-yard length of rayon floss. Working from the back to the front, bring the floss through the center of the circle. Wrap the floss once around the circle and back through the center. Continue to wrap the floss around the circle, making eight sections. Use two strands of floss to blanket-stitch the head to the center top of the front body.

To make antennae, thread the chenille stem through the center back of the head. Trim to the desired length and place a bead on each end. Twist the chenille ends to hold the beads in place.

To make the scissors pocket, center the 2¼×3" teal rectangle on the back of the pincushion. Use teal sewing thread to whipstitch the sides and bottom edges of the rectangle to the pincushion back.♥

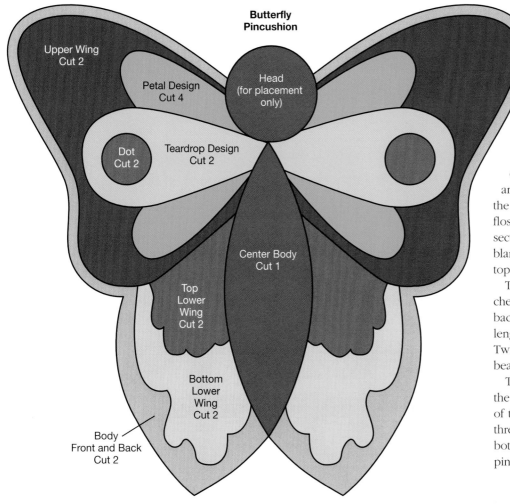

Butterfly Pincushion

Upper Wing
Cut 2

Petal Design
Cut 4

Head
(for placement only)

Dot
Cut 2

Teardrop Design
Cut 2

Center Body
Cut 1

Top
Lower
Wing
Cut 2

Bottom
Lower
Wing
Cut 2

Body
Front and Back
Cut 2

Rug Hooking Basics

If you're new to hooking, Donna Lovelady offers this crash course to help you get started:

1 Always start by hooking the outline of your design; then go back and fill it in. If your design is round, follow the curves. If it's square, work horizontally or vertically. After you've hooked your design, hook a line of background around each design motif to firm up the lines.

2 To begin hooking, insert your hook into the top of the burlap. Hold the wool strip in your other hand under the burlap (Diagram 1).

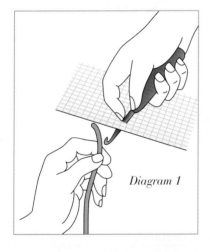

Diagram 1

3 Grasp the wool strip with the hook, and pull the end through the top of the burlap (Diagram 2).

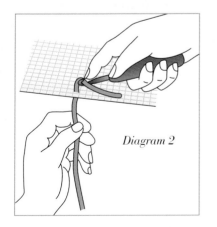

Diagram 2

4 Skip two burlap threads, insert your hook into the burlap again, and pull the wool up to form your first loop (Diagram 3).

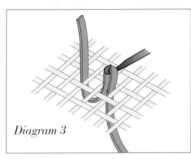

Diagram 3

Since it isn't a loose end, you'll form a loop. The width of your wool strip determines the height of the loop; your loop should be as high as the strip is wide. Continue in this manner until the strip is finished. Make nice, even loops without twisting the wool. When you make a new loop, the last hole will automatically tighten—the pressure of the loops against each other holds them in place. As you work, be careful not to cross over previous stitches.

5 When you finish the first wool strip, bring the ends to the top of the burlap and trim them to the same height as the loops (Diagram 4). After you steam your piece, these ends will be invisible. You can trim them as you go or all at once when the piece is finished.

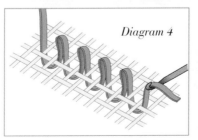

Diagram 4

6 Begin a new strip in the same hole where you just ended. That way, you'll have the same thickness of wool in each hole. It's not necessary to completely use up each strip of wool. If you need to change colors, just bring the end to the top, trim it, and start a new color strip.

7 When you start a new row of strips, always skip about two threads. This will prevent you from hooking your piece too tightly, which will cause it to roll when you remove it from the frame. Hooking tightly can work to your advantage when you're making a pillow, a doll, or anything else that's stuffed. That's because the stuffing will cause the rows of hooking to spread out a bit; tight loops will prevent too much spreading, keeping the burlap from showing.

8 Turn your piece over frequently to make sure it's smooth and has no loose ends. If you spot problems, correct them before continuing. Catching your mistakes early will save you from having to rip out many loops and repeat your work. Don't worry if you spot gaps in the back. But, if you find an opening in the front, go back and fill it in with new loops.

9 When you've finished hooking the entire project, trim any remaining ends. Then, place your piece facedown with a damp towel on top and steam until flat. For larger pieces, like rugs, you may want to use the steam machine at your local dry cleaner. ♥

Sources

Victorian Splendor, pages 6–23:

Aldik *(all pre-lit Christmas trees and artificial greenery throughout the book)*: 800/243-9627; www.aldik.com.

Art Accents *(tiny holeless beads)*: 877/733-8989; www.artaccents.net.

Bucilla *(gold-tone purse clasp)*: 800/842-4197; www.bucilla.com.

Department 56 *(purchased ornaments throughout the book)*: 800/348-3749; www.dept56.com.

Lina G *(8mm pearl trim, vintage flowers, berries, velvet leaves, vintage sequin-beaded leaves, gold coin fringe, gold metallic trims)*: 805/772-7759; www.trimsandribbons.com.

Midwest of Cannon Falls *(purchased ornaments throughout the book)*: 800/776-2075; www.midwestofcannonfalls.com.

Mill Hill *(seed and bugle beads)*: 608/754-9466; www.millhill.com.

National Nonwovens *(wool felt)*: 413/527-3445; www.nationalnonwovens.com.

Prym-Dritz Corporation *(fringes, Hollywood trim, 2½" half ball cover buttons, straight pins)*: 864/576-5050; www.dritz.com.

Wrights *(wired ribbon)*: 800/628-9362; www.wrights.com.

Gifts of the Magi, pages 24–41:

Art Accents *(tiny holeless glass marbles)*: See listing, *above.*

Artistic Wire *(gold wire)*: 630/530-7567; www.artisticwire.com.

Delta Technical Coatings *(Delta Renaissance Foil Gold Kit)*: 800/423-4135; www.deltacrafts.com.

Lina G *(gold metallic trim, gold coin fringe)*: See listing *above.*

Loose Ends *(silk shimmer organza)*: 503/390-2348; www.looseends.com.

Krylon *(Short Cuts gold leaf paint pen)*: 800/457-9566; www.krylon.com.

Plaid Enterprises *(Mod Podge)*: 800/842-4197; www.plaidonline.com.

Roman, Inc. *(Fontanini Nativities)*: 800/540-4754; www.roman.com.

The Little Fox Factory *(cookie cutters: King #1 73-41, King #2 73-42, King #3 73-43, Camel 82-301, and Elephant 89-100)*: To order a catalog, send a S.A.S.E. to The Little Fox Factory, 931 Marion Road, Bacyrus, OH 44820; 419/562-5420, www.thelittlefoxfactory.com.

Ho-Ho-Homespun, pages 42–57:

Artistic Wire *(gold wire)*: See listing *below left.*

Duncan Enterprises *(Aleene's Platinum Bond 7800 adhesive)*: 800/438-6226, www.duncancrafts.com.

C.M. Offray & Sons *(ribbon)*: www.offray.com.

Polyform Products Co. *(Sculpey III polymer clay)*: www.sculpey.com.

Santa's Workshop, pages 58–67:

National Nonwovens *(wool felt)*: See listing *above.*

Polyform Products Co. *(Sculpey III polymer clay)*: See listing *above.*

Shrinky Dinks *(Shrinky Dinks Frosted Ruff n' Ready shrinkable plastic)*: 262-966-0305; www.shrinkydinks.com.

Cedar Lodge, pages 68–79:

American Art Clay Co., Inc. *(tooling foil)*: 800/374-1600; www.amaco.com.

Delta Technical Coatings *(Delta Ceramcoat Acrylic Paints and Gleams paint)*: See listing *left.*

Duncan Enterprises *(Aleene's All Purpose Primer)*: See listing *above.*

Kreative Foam *(foam fish)*: www.kreativefoam.com.

Frosty Friends, pages 104–121:

Warm Company *(quilt batting)*: 800/234-9276; www.warmcompany.com.

National Nonwovens *(wool felt)*: See listing *left.*

Kurt S. Adler *(purchased ornaments)*: www.kurtadler.com.

Gift Ideas, pages 148–156:

Loose Ends *(metallic silk shimmer organza)*: See listing *left.*

National Nonwovens *(wool felt)*: See listing *left.*

DMC Corporation *(embroidery floss)*: 973/589-0606; www.dmc-usa.com.

Better Homes and Gardens® Creative Collection™

CHRISTMAS
FROM THE HEART.

Creative Director	Patricia Church Podlasek

Executive Editor	Mary L. Heaton
Senior Editor	Nancy Wyatt
Food Editor	Julia Martinusen
Associate Art Director	Carrie Topp
Editorial Assistant	Cathy Celsi
Contributing Writers	Laura Collins, Rhonda Matus
Contributing Illustrators	Glenda Aldrich, Barbara Gordon, Chris Neubauer Graphics
Photo Stylist	Patty Crawford
Prop and Photo Assistants	Holly Raibikis, Kenneth Seiling
Food Stylist	Jill Lust

Vice President, Publishing Director	William R. Reed

Group Publisher	Maureen Ruth
Consumer Product Marketing Director	Ben Jones
Consumer Product Marketing Manager	Karrie Nelson
Business Manager	Kie Lin
Production Manager	Douglas M. Johnston
Book Production Managers	Pam Kvitne, Marjorie J. Schenkelberg
Assistant to the Publisher	Cheryl Eckert

MEREDITH PUBLISHING GROUP

Publishing Group President	Stephen M. Lacy
Magazine Group President	Jerry Kaplan
Corporate Solutions	Michael Brownstein
Creative Services	Ellen de Lathouder
Manufacturing	Bruce Heston
Consumer Marketing	Karla Jeffries
Finance and Administration	Max Runciman

Meredith CORPORATION

Chairman and CEO	William T. Kerr
Chairman of the Executive Committee	E.T. Meredith III

For editorial questions, please write:
**BETTER HOMES AND GARDENS®
CHRISTMAS FROM THE HEART®, Volume 11**
1716 Locust Street, Des Moines, IA 50309-3023.

 Member HOBBY INDUSTRY ASSOCIATION

 Crafts. Discover life's little pleasures.

Contributing Photographers

Marcia Cameron: *Pages 22, 40–41, 104, 116, 120–121, and 158.*

Mike Dieter: *Pages 122–131, 133–147, and 160.*

Scott Little: *Pages 2, 6–14, 17–23, 24–29, 32, 34–36, 38, 80–89, 91–93, 95–96, 98, 100–101, 103, 105–109, 112, and 114.*

Perry Struse: *Pages 3, 42–47, 49, 51–53, 55, and 68–79.*

Steve Struse: *Pages 4, 58–62, 64, 67, 148–151, 153–154, and 156.*

Cover Photograph:
Perry Struse

On the twelfth day of Christmas my true love sent to me twelve drummers drumming...

—*English traditional carol (author unknown, words and tune handed down from generation to generation)*